INFORMATION SYSTEMS AND
PERFORMANCE MEASURES IN SCHOOLS

INFORMATION SYSTEMS AND PERFORMANCE MEASURES IN SCHOOLS

James S. Coleman
and
Nancy L. Karweit

Educational Technology Publications
Englewood Cliffs, New Jersey 07632

Printed in the United States of America.

Library of Congress Catalog Card Number:
72-79547

International Standard Book Number:
0-87778-038-2.

First Printing.

THE AUTHORS

James S. Coleman is professor of Social Relations at The Johns Hopkins University. Nancy L. Karweit is research scientist with the Center for Social Organization of Schools at Johns Hopkins. The authors are consultants to The Rand Corporation, Santa Monica, California.

PREFACE

This investigation began as a study of administrative data systems in education, with the aim of designing computerized systems which would facilitate such administration, and also provide data for research purposes. As we progressed, however, several points became apparent.

First, the principal problems in schools did not arise from the current organization of data systems, and would not be solved by the introduction of computerized systems. Minor gains might be made, but this seemed hardly sufficient to warrant devotion of staff attention and educational resources to such computerization. There have been a number of projects involving computerization of administrative functions, some of which are reviewed in Chapter Two. These have often been mildly successful, but they seem not to have brought important benefits to school functioning, with the exception of possibly better student scheduling.

Second, at one point in the investigation it became clear that the greatest value of such computerized systems would occur in extremely large school districts, in which the number of students and staff is so large as to overwhelm the administrative mechanism. It became apparent that automated data systems in these districts might merely allow an already depersonalized system to become more so, and to grow into even larger units through amalgamation (sometimes justified in terms of "administrative efficiency," or to spread capital costs of computer administrative equipment).

Third, our aim of "providing data for research purposes" seemed also irrelevant to school functioning. Few research results ever find their way back to school districts and schools to affect decisions. Their principal destination is scholarly publication, and they often remain there.

In reaction to these points, there emerged a different conception of data systems in education, and of the educational system generally. This is the conception of many parties with legitimate interests in education, both within the formal organization of school districts and outside, and of an information system that would aid the decisions of these various interested parties. The resulting conception and design is one which bears little similarity to management information systems that are designed to serve the needs of hierarchical organizations. It is explicitly designed as an information system for multiple users, from parents and children to legislators, and including persons in the organizational structure of schools, from teachers to superintendents. It is designed for the *emerging pluralistic structure of American education,* in which all parties to education make responsible choices; it is designed to aid in the emergence of such a pluralistic structure, and to aid in such responsible choice.

J.S.C. and N.L.K.

ACKNOWLEDGMENTS

The survey of information systems for pupil personnel records was greatly aided by a number of persons in school districts in the Los Angeles area. We would like especially to thank Dr. George K. Drake, principal, Santa Monica High School; Mr. Jonie Lewis, coordinator of guidance, Santa Monica High School; Dr. Julius Steir, director of research, Santa Monica School District; Mr. Robert B. Case, principal, Crenshaw High School; Dr. Clark Cosgrove, assistant director, Test and Evaluation Division, Los Angeles City Schools; Mr. Henry O. Dyck, administrative coordinator, Division of Secondary Education, Los Angeles City Schools; Mr. Bernard Victorino, Data Processing Project, Crenshaw High School; Dr. Isabel Dible, Director of Elementary Instruction, Beverly Hills; Dr. John French, principal, Beverly Vista School; Mr. Lawrence D. Lynch, assistant principal, Beverly Hills High School; and Mr. Ronald Goll and Mr. Dean F. Waters of the Norwalk-La Mirada Unified School District.

In addition, we would like to thank Mr. Larry Nebble of Remote Computing Corporation and Mr. Victor Sampson of Call-A-Computer Corporation for information about current and proposed time-sharing computer systems.

The writing of this book was sponsored by The Rand Corporation as a part of its domestic research program.

CONTENTS

Preface   *ix*

Acknowledgments   *xi*

1. A General Overview of Information for Educational Decisions   *3*

2. Educational Data Systems   *11*

3. The Design of Information Systems for Multi-Level Decisions   *32*

4. Implementation of a Multi-Level Information System   *54*

5. School Performance Measures   *82*

References   *117*

Index   *121*

Selected List of Rand Books   *129*

LIST OF FIGURES

Figure 1:   Data Linkage   64

Figure 2:   Communication Flow   67

Figure 3:   Remote Computing Network   76

Figure 4:   Linked Test Scores with
               Common Mean and Variance   93

Figure 5:   Linked Test Scores with
               Increasing Mean and Variance   97

Figure 6·   Equivalence Between Standard
               Scores and Percentile Scores   100

LIST OF TABLES

Table 1:   Types of Information
for Use in
Educational Decision-Making   6

Table 2:   Activity List via Computer   23

Table 3:   Modes of Computer Access   29

Table 4:   Generation and Maintenance of Data
Necessary for Educational Decisions
Related to Student Performance   37

Table 5:   Grade Equivalents   91

Table 6:   Reading Achievement Test Scores
by Percentile   98

Table 7:   Reading Achievement Test Scores
by Standard Scores   101

INFORMATION SYSTEMS AND
PERFORMANCE MEASURES IN SCHOOLS

CHAPTER ONE

A GENERAL OVERVIEW OF INFORMATION FOR EDUCATIONAL DECISIONS

This book presents an examination of data systems in education. Its aim is to provide a framework through which such data systems can aid educational decisions. In the past, records in schools have been maintained as physical files, in a form which allowed easy access for the main administrative use to which the records were put. As schools and school systems have grown in size, however, the need for more efficient handling of these records has become pressing, and many schools and school districts are developing computerized data systems.

With these computerized administrative data systems, it becomes possible to use records for many purposes other than the administrative use for which they are maintained. Because the records are electronically rather than physically stored, they can be sorted, aggregated, merged, and subjected to statistical data reduction in many ways for many purposes.

In particular, such facilities make it possible to erase the artificial distinction between administrative uses of information and research or evaluation uses. Administrative uses of information are uses for decisions, ranging from decisions about individual cases to general policy decisions. Research and evaluation in schools is also carried out to aid in such decisions. However, research or evaluation has ordinarily required collection of special data on a "project" basis, at large costs and with uncertain value for policy decisions. The opportunity created by computerized data systems is to integrate research and administrative uses of information to aid in educational decisions at all levels.

Apart from this opportunity, created by change in technology, there are two factors which create a pressure for broader uses of educational information than in the past. The first is increased consumer power in education, as parents and parent groups exert pressures for release of information previously restricted to educational administrators. The second is increased focus on the *outputs of education,* the actual performance of children, rather than solely the inputs of resources into schools. These two factors together are creating increasing demand by persons outside schools for broad evaluative uses of information that previously served only internal administrative uses in schools.

But problems exist in realizing this aim. First, the data systems must be appropriately designed from the outset to bring the power of the information to bear on education decisions. There are numerous kinds of decisions to be made, and the system must be designed in cognizance of these different kinds of decisions. Second, different parties in education have different interests, and there may be conflicts in the use of information to implement these interests. Information is power, and access to information in educational data systems affects the power of various parties in the educational process. Differently designed systems will place information in the hands of different parties, and it is necessary to recognize the power implications of various systems. Third, there are numerous other considerations in the design of computer data systems: cost, ease of use, flexibility, and adaptability to new uses; compatibility with instructional uses of computers; and modularity of design to allow incremental introduction of a new system.

This book will focus on these problems in the design of educational data systems for administrative and research-evaluation purposes.

The Interested Parties to Education

To begin examination of data systems in education, it is perhaps most useful to begin from the "wrong way 'round," identifying the interested parties and examining the interests of each and the kinds of decisions of each. Only after this will we look at data systems in schools as they currently exist and as they can come to exist under existing computer technology.

There are a number of interested parties in education who make decisions that affect educational outcomes. For present purposes, it is useful to distinguish the following interested parties: parent, child, teacher, principal, superintendent, state government, and federal government, neglecting finer distinctions, such as state education department as distinct from state legislators. These different parties are interested in different kinds of information—in information about performance of particular students, types of students, or students in general; in information about effectiveness of particular programs (or curricula, teachers, or schools), or in effectiveness of certain types of programs, curricula, teachers, and schools. Each has an interest in access to certain kinds of information (for example, parents have an interest in access to information about the effectiveness of a particular teacher or school), and each has an interest in restricting access to certain information (for example, superintendents have an interest in restricting access to information on school-by-school measures of student performance, or parents have an interest in restricting access to their child's measures of performance).

To gain some idea of the kinds of decisions that each party makes, and the kind of information useful to him in making these decisions, it is useful first to describe the general class of decisions which concern us here: decisions about *the exposure of students to possibly effective educational environments.* Within this class, some decisions concern individual students, some concern students with particular characteristics, some concern all students. Some concern particular educational environments, some concern certain types of environments, and some concern performance apart from the specific environment. These classes of decisions are described in Table 1, which shows nine kinds of information about performance.

Table 1

Types of Information for Use in Educational Decision-Making

	Performance by:		
	Individual Students	Characteristics of Students	All Students
Particular Environment	1	2	3
Characteristics of Environment	4	5	6
Independent of Environment	7	8	9

In Table 1, the label "particular environment" refers to a specific case: a certain teacher, Jane Jones; a certain curriculum, the PSSC physics curriculum; a certain school, P.S. 86. The label "characteristics of environment" refers to variables that characterize the educational environment: teacher characteristics, class size, etc. A similar distinction concerning students exists between the first two columns of the table. The cells represent given types of information upon which decisions can be based. For example, information about the performance of students with high initial achievement in physics, in a specific physics course with the PSSC curriculum, is information of type 2 in the table.

The term "research" is ordinarily confined to information of types 5 and 6, showing effects of environmental characteristics on student performance. "Evaluation" is sometimes used in the same way, but more often refers to information of types 2 and 3: effectiveness of particular programs (often experimental or demonstration programs) on performance of students in general, or the performance of particular groups of students (e.g., students with initially low reading scores). What is important to recognize, however, is that these types of information constitute only a fraction of the information on student performance necessary for educational decisions. Thus to focus on research and evaluation, as ordinarily defined, without initial attention to the types of decisions made by the various interested parties, artificially restricts the frame of reference.

The decisions of state and federal governments in education are decisions about funding types of programs, both in their impact on students in general, and in their impact on students with particular characteristics. For these decisions, they need information of types 5 and 6 in Table 1.

Decisions of school boards and school superintendents are also concerned with this general knowledge about effects of types of school environments on students, but they are also very much concerned with information of types 2 and 3. Their decisions are a mixture of decisions about particular environments and general types of environment. They are often decisions about whether to continue a particular program, or a particular curriculum, or whether to make a given person a school principal; but they are also decisions about whether to institute a program with given characteristics, what types of teachers to hire, or what kinds of physical facilities to construct. The information they need for these latter types of decisions (information of types 5 and 6) ordinarily transcends their districts, for the information base in their districts may not contain the relevant experience.

Principals' decisions ordinarily concern particular programs, particular teachers, and particular teaching aids, so that the information they need is of types 2 and 3: information about the effectiveness of those particular learning environments in their school—information which will help them decide whether to continue or to stop the program in question. In some cases, their decisions concern individual students, requiring information of types 1, 4, or 7, to decide on the disposition of students who present special problems.

Teachers and counselors most often make decisions about individual students, and require information on performance of individual students, of types 1, 4, and 7. Counselors are also concerned with decisions about the probable performance of certain types of students in certain types of environments (e.g., what types of students perform best with certain types of teachers, or what types of students are successful in certain kinds of colleges), requiring information of type 5. Teachers also make decisions about the performance of certain types of students in a particular environment (e.g., class discussion or class projects, drill or games), for which information of type 2 is necessary. More broadly, teachers also need information of types 5, 6, and 8 as a background for planning everyday activities. This general information is the sort that teachers get or should get during their training.

Parents and children are first of all interested in the individual child's performance, information of type 7; but in making decisions about what school to attend, or what teacher to try to get, they need information of types 1, 2, 3, and 4. Insofar as choices of parent and child are expanded, through allowing a greater range of choices of schedules and even of schools, information of types 5, 6, and 8 as well is necessary for making these choices wisely.

From this assessment of decisions at various levels, requiring various types of information, it is clear that any data system which would satisfy these needs must be both technically and administratively complex. The technical complexity lies in the fact that raw performance measures of students will not serve most of these information functions. To know the effectiveness of educational environments for performance requires detailed statistical analyses of the student performance under different educational environments. The administrative complexity lies in the question of control over and access to various types of information. Information cannot be totally controlled at a given level within the educational hierarchy, for it would become useful only for those at that level; and it cannot be wholly contained within the school organizations themselves, for it would be of no use to federal and state governments or to parents and children. To obtain general information of types 5, 6, and 8 requires information from many school districts.

This examination of types of information and levels of decision-making describes the dimensions of the problem. The next section gives an overview of the characteristics of emerging computerized data systems in schools and school districts. These data systems have on the whole been developed merely to automate the existing uses of school records, to aid school staff and administrators. But despite the limited uses for which they have been designed, they constitute the nucleus from which information systems to serve the various levels of decisions described above can be developed.

CHAPTER TWO

EDUCATIONAL DATA SYSTEMS

Procedures in Existing Data Systems

The information about current data systems given in this chapter comes from interviews with school administrators of several school districts in the Los Angeles area and from available literature. Although administrative data systems entail collection and maintenance of data for all facets of a school district's activities, this survey concentrates exclusively on pupil personnel data systems. There are six major areas included in pupil personnel systems: scheduling, attendance reporting, grade reporting, standardized test reporting, career and college counseling, and master file maintenance.

The data bases maintained by the various districts for the pupil personnel systems are very similar. Maintenance procedures differ, however, according to the availability of types of data processing equipment.

Scheduling

The process of matching subjects, students, instructors, and classrooms within a school is called building the school schedule. For secondary schools, there are currently three types of scheduling used in American public schools: (1) class scheduling, in which each class group is scheduled together, and remains as a class group throughout all (or nearly all) school classes for the semester or year; (2) individual scheduling, in which each student follows a distinct schedule, and has a different set of classmates for each class; and (3) flexible scheduling, in which the school day is not arranged into periods of equal and fixed length, but into smaller modules, with a given class (say English literature) consisting of one or more contiguous modules, which may differ in length and position among different days of the week. Very few schools currently use flexible scheduling; there are many that use individual scheduling and many that use class scheduling.

At the elementary school, children in most schools have a single teacher for all or most of the day. Consequently, at elementary levels, scheduling is ordinarily done with relative ease.

The computer scheduling programs are designed to be used for individual scheduling, although some may be used also for flexible scheduling.

The construction of a schedule with the aid of a computer may be approached in several ways. A master schedule assigning rooms, teachers, subjects, and times may first be built and then students may be scheduled within that framework. Or the subjects, instructors, classrooms, and students can simultaneously be considered in order to produce a school schedule in one process.

Making the school schedule is a tedious and time-consuming task. The school principal or other school administrator can easily spend at least one month and as many as six months in drawing up the schedule. To reduce the time involved, several computer programs have been developed to accomplish the sectioning or registering of students. Several systems have been designed to perform the entire scheduling procedure. For example, the Stanford School Scheduling System, developed through the Department of Education at Stanford University, has been used by many school systems to build a master schedule and then register students. Since most of the schools which use the computer in scheduling first build a master schedule and then let the computer register students, this is the organization presented in the discussion which follows.

Master Scheduling. The master schedule designates the time, room number, and teacher for every course taught in the school. Drawing up the master schedule requires matching teacher, room, and time constraints. Due to the large numbers of input parameters, direct solution of the problem is not likely. Instead, the computer simulates the trial-and-error method of the human scheduler in arriving at possible teacher-room-time student assignments. Although usage of such programs is possible, the more widespread practice entails drawing up the master and student schedules separately. For most school districts using the computer in master scheduling, the computer provides guidelines for the human scheduler and not the master schedule itself. In some instances, student course requests and maximum course size data are inputs to a program, which then provides the number of sections needed for each course. A print-out of the number of requests by all pairs of courses is also printed. With this matrix it is possible to see that, for example, thirty students who want to take senior orchestra also want to take physics. Knowing this cross-demand for courses can prevent many potential conflicts in construction of the master schedule. Using these guidelines, the human scheduler then makes out the master schedule. He writes the schedule onto a coding sheet for keypunching. Each punched card contains the name of the course, the time and place of meeting, the teacher's name, and possibly any prerequisite courses. A computer program reads in the master schedule and, as one output, prints the schedule for each individual teacher. Then, if any teacher's schedule is too heavily concentrated in one part of the day, the master schedule can be adjusted in light of this fact. In summary, scheduling is still done by a person, with the computer providing useful guidelines in its formulation.

Student Scheduling. Student scheduling is the procedure which registers and schedules students for courses offered by the school. This procedure occurs at least once a year, and in school districts where course changes may take place at the second semester, it occurs twice a year. The inputs to student scheduling are the individual student course requests and the school's master schedule. From this process, each student receives a schedule, each teacher obtains class rosters, and the central office receives a master class schedule with names of students in each class.

Student scheduling entails matching student course requests with the offerings of the master schedule. In elementary schools, where the students typically remain with the same teacher in the same classrooms for all courses, manual systems are widely used. In this case students are placed in homerooms and the schedule for all students in that room is the same.

At the high school level, many systems use either partially or totally automated systems for scheduling. In both cases the students receive either a mark-sense card or optical scan sheet, with their name and identification code marked on it. On this document, the student indicates his course requests for the next year. In one partially automated system that was examined, the procedures which were followed are these: The registration card is prepared by counselor and student. Meanwhile, class cards for available places in each course have been prepared (automatically from the master schedule) and placed in bins. To register a student in a particular course, a course card is removed from the requested course bin. Printing all the course cards and student's identification card provides the schedule for individual students. Printing all the request cards filed for the particular course provides the class roster.

Many systems use a partially automated system similar to the one described above. There has been, however, a proliferation of computer student scheduling programs in the past five years, and many systems have tried them out. The satisfaction with the computer student scheduling appears high; in the school districts we interviewed, only one was unhappy enough with the results to abandon this method completely. If a school district does not have its own computer, it either rents time commercially for scheduling or borrows time from some cooperating computer center.

To use a computer scheduling program, the student requests and the master schedule must be placed on machine-readable documents. These are then input to the student scheduling program, which produces a variety of outputs. Included are: (1) student conflicts, (2) individual student schedules, and (3) updated master schedule with the number of students assigned to each class.

Ideally the first run produces conflict-free schedules for 90-95 percent of the students. The human scheduler must then rearrange the schedule to reduce remaining conflicts. Usually three iterations through the program produce a satisfactory schedule.

Attendance Reporting

Attendance reporting in secondary schools is ordinarily carried out by the homeroom teacher, who transmits the names of absent students to the attendance officer. Master lists of absent students are then distributed to all teachers. Tallies of number of times absent are recorded on a student's report card and in his permanent folder. Monthly school-wide attendance reports are tallied for average daily attendance reports to the state.

In addition, there are readmission procedures to be followed after a student's absence. In a typical procedure, upon bringing a note from home explaining his absence, the student is readmitted to school. He then takes a readmission slip to every class, to be signed by the class teacher.

In one partially automated system that was surveyed, at the beginning of the year each homeroom teacher receives for each student expected in his home room an IBM card containing the student's name. When a student is absent, the homeroom teacher sends that student's card to data processing, where a master absentee list is printed and distributed to teachers.

The data center and the school are usually not physically located in the same place. Consequently, transportation time may prohibit quick distribution of the absentee list. There are several data collection devices which may be installed at the school and which can transmit data (via phone lines) to a remote computer. For example, one device can read and transmit data recorded on punched cards, mark-sense cards, or mark-sense sheets. One school system (Oakland Schools in Pontiac, Michigan) utilizes Touch Tone telephones and inserts an individual card dialer for each absent pupil. Another school (a junior high in Baltimore,

Maryland) uses a remote card reader to transmit the attendance data and a typewriter terminal for receiving the lists of absent students.

The virtue of using a completely automated system is the elimination of the hand recording of both the daily and other attendance reports. Daily attendance data for each student are automatically recorded in his master file and, from these data, attendance profiles, irregular attendance reports, and average daily attendance reports may be generated.

Grade Reporting

Every teacher gives grades and records results of tests for each student in a gradebook. At certain intervals these grades are averaged and reports of each student's progress sent to his parents and recorded in his cumulative folder. Students may be ranked by their grade average; special lists such as honor roll, incompletes, or failures may be made; the distribution of grades given by each teacher may be provided.

In a manual system, each student's report card is circulated to all his teachers, who record his grade for that class. This same grade information is hand posted in the student's cumulative folder either by a homeroom teacher or a clerk.

Partially automated systems eliminate circulation of the grade reports among teachers. Instead, each teacher marks the grade on a machine-readable document, and returns these forms to the data processing center. A student's grade reports from his teachers are collated and his final report card is printed both on a report form for his parents and on a gummed label to affix to his cumulative folder.

In a completely automated system the student answers

his test questions on a form which the computer can read. Test scoring and recording of the grade are done by the computer, which stores this information on tape or disk. From these data, averages are calculated by the computer, which periodically gives the teacher reports on student test averages. At report time, the teacher uses these reports from the computer to assign grades to students for that reporting period. The teacher reports grades on a machine-readable document as in the partially automated system. (It is possible also to have grade reports directly made by the computer from test averages, if the teacher prefers that the grade depend solely on these.) The report cards for distribution to parents are then generated. At the same time the student's master file is updated with these current grades. Several special reports may optionally be available as part of the grade reporting process, such as (1) list of failures, (2) list of honor roll students, (3) list of students with incompletes, and (4) rank of students by grade point average.

Standardized Testing

Some state governments require that a standardized testing program be carried out by each district in the state. Other states have a testing program that is voluntary for districts. In addition, most districts have their own standardized testing schedule, resulting in a large number of tests to be scored, recorded, and analyzed.

A manual system for standardized test reporting requires a human grader to mark each item by comparing it with the scoring key. Scores are accumulated and then recorded for each student. School-wide averages, if obtained, would entail writing down and then summing all students' scores. Such manual procedures are highly tedious, and lead to frequent errors; they are seldom used by districts.

The procedures for collecting and maintaining standardized test data are very similar in the systems surveyed, which are partially automated systems. In this system, test packets containing the test and answer sheet are distributed to each student. These answer sheets have the student's name and identification code precoded on them. After test-taking, the tests are sent back to the test supplier for scoring and recording. The results are supplied as (1) gummed labels with individual student scores, (2) school averages, standard deviations, and (3) district averages, standard deviations.

The virtue of a completely automated system for standardized test reporting is the accessibility of previous test reports, so that over-time comparisons become possible. Tests are administered and scored in a manner similar to the semi-automated procedures. The results are stored electronically as well as in the cumulative folder, thus permitting the possibility of more easily retrieving and utilizing these data.

Career and College Counseling

Frequently the information on which students base their post-high school plans is obtained informally, in a non-systematic manner. The high school does provide career and college information, through such programs as "career nights" or "college days" in which representatives talk to the students. Additionally, job description pamphlets and college catalogues are available for the students. In many schools, post-college plans are discussed with counselors or in home rooms throughout school careers.

Counseling the student about his post-high school plans often requires aptitude and interest tests. The scoring and recording of these tests is similar to the procedure for standardized achievement test reporting.

Currently, there are several projects underway which are utilizing computer assistance in counseling. A central feature of these systems is a computer library or data base of career and college information along with methods for its retrieval. One career guidance system asks the student about his interests and post-high school plans and then lists possible jobs matching his characteristics. Then the student may request additional information about any of these jobs.

The College Entrance Examination Board is developing one such system, called the College Locator Service, to give students information on which to base their selection of a college.

Currently the student has very little data on which to decide which college to attend. He may read what the college chooses to tell him in its catalogue, or he may talk to students attending that college. On the other hand, the colleges gain quite detailed information about applicants from their high school records and College Entrance Examination Board tests. A college locator service, by providing substantive information about the college's performance, would help redress this imbalance of information between the colleges and their applicants.

Master File Maintenance

The depository for the output of all these procedures is the student master history file, called his cumulative record. Typically this record is a manila folder with space allocated for recording grades, standardized scores, and background information of the student. State law may require that such a folder be kept and specify the minimum contents of this folder.

Most school districts store this master file as a physical record and manually update their students' master records. Thus attendance data, names, and grades earned in courses are all manually transcribed into the student's record. Some automation of the preparation of data to be inserted in the record has been carried out. For instance, test scores are printed by a computer on gummed labels instead of being handwritten. But these same scores still must be affixed to the cumulative record, a manual process.

There are a few examples of master records stored electronically, either on magnetic tape or disk. When the student's master file is stored in this manner, updating his file becomes a part of the report generation process. Manual transcription of the results of an activity (e.g., grade reporting, standardized testing) to the master file is eliminated, since the master record is automatically updated when the results of the activity are recorded. With a fully automated data system, information is added to the student's folder as it becomes available, not at the end of the year or some other arbitrary update time. Thus the student's folder always contains current information, and accurately reflects the current status of the student. The cumulative file, which in most schools at present is the depository of historical information about the student, has the possibility of becoming the data base for continual monitoring of a student's progress.

One school district surveyed had placed the most recent seven semesters of each student's cumulative record on a magnetic tape. Computer programs were written to scan the tape for persons fitting particular characteristics—for instance, location of all those junior year students who had not completed the health course requirement—and the list of persons satisfying this characteristic would be printed. The district had not developed a general information retrieval system, but wrote a new program to search for each specific characteristic.

To implement each of the areas of work described above with the use of a computer would entail a certain set of activities. While the activities will differ somewhat for different school systems, it is useful to lay out in tabular form the detailed activities necessary to carry out each of the areas of work via computer procedures. Table 2 shows for five of the six areas of work described above (excluding career and college counseling, for which no standard methods of computer use have been developed) the transactions involved in carrying out the activity via computer.

Modes of Computer Access

Nearly all the computer systems that currently exist in schools operate with a central computer, located at a district or regional office (or in rare cases, at a high school), to which jobs are submitted, inserted in a schedule, and then run in scheduled sequence. However, recent developments have allowed new modes of computer access, and it is useful to examine briefly the differences in mode of operation this can allow.

It is useful to examine the various modes of access to a computer according to two dimensions: access may be either interactive or noninteractive, and it may involve simultaneous access by more than one user or exclusive access by a single user. Table 3 classifies computer systems by these two dimensions.

Noninteractive access means that the computer user and the computer do not have any two-way communication

2a Creation and Maintenance of Master File

Activity	Input	Output	Frequency	Description
Create master file	1 card/student	1 record/student	once a year	Creates initial record for student, enters school code, student's name, sex, grade, date of birth, home address, and other background data.
Add or delete students from master file	1 card/student	updated master	as needed	Adds new students to the file and disenrolls students no longer attending that school.
Normal file maintenance	1 record/student	updated master	20 times/year (grade report data at 5-week intervals and standardized tests twice/year)	Output from grade reporting and standardized testing are recorded on master file.
Print complete file	master file	maximum of 40 lines/student	2 times/year	Complete listing of all entries in the master file. Maximum of 40 lines if all data present on student from K-12th grades.
Print partial file	master file and output requests	3 lines/student	20 times/year	Listing of selected portions of the master file.

2b Scheduling

Activity	Input	Output	Frequency	Description
Record student requests	1 document/ student	1 record/ student	2 times/year	Students record their course requests either on sense cards, optical scan sheets or coding forms.
Edit student requests	1 record/ student	8 lines/ student	2 times/year	Student requests are checked against course offerings; errors due to improper course number, lack of prerequisite, sex or grade restriction are indicated.
Print tally	1 record/ student	1 line/ course	2 times/year	Tally of number of requests per course is printed.
Print cross tally	1 record/ course	30 lines/ course	2 times/year	Cross tally of course requests printed. To reduce the large volume of output, probably would include only courses with fewer than 50 requested.
Enter master schedule	1 record/ course	1 record/ course	2 times/year	Build working file containing master schedule.
Assignment, simulations, and final run		15 lines/ conflict	6 times/year	Prints conflicts.

2b Scheduling (continued)

Activity	Input	Output	Frequency	Description
Revise master schedule and individual student schedules		3 lines/ student	6 times/year	Adjustments to master schedule and individual student schedules are made.
Print student schedules—1		8 lines/ student	2 times/year	Prints student schedules giving course name, course number, teacher name, room number.
Print student schedules—2		3 lines/ student	2 times/year	Prints abbreviated student schedules on gummed labels for student use.
Print class lists	student schedules	1 line/ student/ course	2 times/year	Prints class enrollment by course number.

2c Attendance Data

Activity	Input	Output	Frequency	Description
Generate attendance reporting document	student master file	1 document/ student	once a year	Cards or optical scan sheets are generated for each student.
List daily absentees	1 document/ absentee	1 line/absentee (approximately 15 percent absentee rate)	daily, approximately 178 times	Names of absent students along with cumulative days absent are printed.
Print summary reports and update master file	attendance file	summary/ student, summary/ school	monthly	Attendance profiles for each student are printed as well as summary statistics for the school.

2d Report Cards

Activity	Input	Output	Frequency	Description
Generate grade reporting document	1 record/ student	7 documents/ student	8 times/year	Documents with student's name, course number are generated. May either be punched cards, mark-sense cards or optical scan sheets.
Read, edit, print grades as received	7 documents/ student	7 lines/ student	8 times/year	Grades as received are edited for completeness and listing returned to teachers for corrections.
Correct report cards	1 card/ correction	1 line/ correction (estimate 10 percent error rate)	8 times/year	Correct errors in initial grade reporting.
Print report cards	1 record/ student	20 lines/ student	8 times/year	Print report cards and update master file.
Print grade analysis	1 record/ student		8 times/year	Print distribution of grades for each teacher, print list of failures, print list of honor roll students.

2e Testing

Activity	Input	Output	Frequency	Description
Create test scoring documents	master file	2 cards/ student	2 times/year	Cards or optical scan sheets are prepared by recording necessary student identifiers.
Score tests	2 documents/ student	1 record/ student	2 times/year	Answer sheets are read and recorded.
Generate reports	1 record/ student	1 line/ student	2 times/year	Summary statistics by school and other classifications are printed.
Print gummed labels	1 record/ student	2 lines/ student	2 times/year	Gummed labels with test results are printed.

Table 3

Modes of Computer Access

	Noninteractive	Interactive
Simultaneous access by more than one user	Multi-programming remote batch	Time-sharing
Access by one user	Batch processing	Dedicated system

during the execution of the user's program. The computer may print various data during execution. In addition, the program may include points at which he enters new data. For example, the user may enter a set of students' grades in response to a computer request, and the computer immediately adds these grades to prior grades and prints out the new grade averages to the user. The important distinction between interactive and noninteractive systems is the two-way communication that can occur during program execution in interactive systems.

The other variable used in classifying modes of computer access is the number of users who have access at any one time.

In many computer systems, access to the computer is limited to one user at a time. The computer belongs exclusively to this one user during the execution of his program; other programs do not interrupt its execution. In a noninteractive, one-user system or batch processing system, users typically submit programs to a central computing facility. These jobs are run on the computer in an order established by a computer job scheduler. The turnaround time (time between job submittal and job completion) may be minutes, hours, or longer, but is ordinarily measured in hours, and sometimes in days.

A one-user system can be interactive, as a dedicated system. For instance, while a program is in execution, the computer operator can display registers and alter contents of the computer.

Simultaneity of access refers to systems in which execution of one program is interspersed with the execution of one or more other programs. The computer jumps from program to program, not performing execution of one entire program as a unit, but executing portions of many problems—either to allow interactive capability to a number of users as in time sharing, or to allow more efficient use of different computer components, as in multi-programming. Although multiple user access to the computer may be generally called time-sharing, the term "time-sharing" has come to mean a time-shared computer with interactive remote users. These definitions will be used in the discussion which follows.

> *multiprogramming*—non-remote, noninteractive time-sharing
> *time-sharing system*—remote, interactive time-sharing
> *remote batch*—remote, noninteractive, non-time-sharing, or time-sharing

In *multiprogramming systems*, the users do not interact with their program during its execution. Programs are submitted to a central computing facility where they are run and then retrieved by the user. Swapping of execution of programs is done to maximize machine efficiency.

Time-sharing systems are, on the other hand, interactive. The user through the use of a teletypewriter or equivalent device has the computer at his fingertips and may enter programs, compile them, edit them, enter data, and receive output data. There is a central computer to which the remote users are attached via phone lines and teletypewriters. The user "calls" the computer and then begins entering his program or data on the teletypewriter.

Remote batch users are linked to the computer via phone lines as well. In this mode the remote user requests that a job be run at some time later. The output may be returned to him via messenger, or through his remote terminal, depending on the amount of output and the capability of his terminal. He does not interact with the program during its execution.

Until recently, computers were restricted to access by one user. Even now, most computer installations operate in this mode. However, recent developments in computers and systems programming have made possible simultaneous access by many users, and with appropriate systems programming, an interactive mode. A number of commercial services now offer time-sharing and remote batch operation via telephone lines, with the remote user having a teletypewriter or card reader input, and teletypewriter or line printer output.

A remote station with card reader input, printer output, interactive capability through a typewriter, and magnetic tape and disk file storage at the central computer has effectively the essential capabilities of the central computer directly accessible to the user in time and space. Perhaps equally important, he has capital expenditures only for his terminal equipment, and pays computer costs through user charges.

CHAPTER THREE

THE DESIGN OF INFORMATION SYSTEMS FOR MULTI-LEVEL DECISIONS

Information systems for educational decisions can build upon the data systems currently being implemented in schools, involving the activities described in Chapter Two. There are five principal design problems that must be addressed in doing so:

1. Problems of *location,* arising from differences between the locus at which data are generated, the locus at which the file is maintained, and the locus at which information is needed for decisions.
2. Problems of *control* of and *access* to the information.
3. Problems of *comparability of data* from different schools or different school districts.
4. Problems of *incomplete information*: data not ordinarily obtained or filed for administration purposes, but necessary for decisions of various types.
5. Problems of information *aggregation, analysis,* and *presentation.*

This chapter will examine each of these problems and outline the requirements of a system which will provide information at multiple levels for educational decisions to be made by the various parties concerned.

The Loci at Which Data Are Generated
and Files Are Maintained

Chapter Two examined the various activities involved in generation and maintenance of student information. In general, these data are generated at either the classroom level or at the school level, and files are maintained at the school level. In some cases, individual student records are maintained at the district level, containing selected information from the student record maintained at the school. The automation of student record maintenance will make this pattern more frequent in the future, where computer hardware exists only at the district level. This student information, maintained at the school or district level, is in unaggregated form. Thus, to refer to Table 1, it contains information of type 7 and sometimes 1, useful only for decisions about particular students independent of educational environment, and sometimes in particular environments (e.g., how well a student is doing in a given track).

Student performance data are also maintained in aggregated form at higher levels (district, state), giving information of types 3 and 9 in Table 1. However, so long as these data are not associated with information about the educational environments, they do not provide information of types 4, 5, and 6, which are probably the types of information most broadly needed for decisions, as indicated in Chapter One.

Certain data on student performance are generated at higher levels. Machine-scored tests are ordinarily scored at a district level or higher (and sometimes by an outside service contractor). Information on post-school activities, in education or in occupations, is generated outside the school system, either in college or places of work. Because such data are not generated within the school system, they ordinarily

do not enter educational records, even though they constitute valuable information to the school concerning the
performance of its products, and thus indirectly its own
performance.

In addition to student performance information, other
information is necessary for educational decisions. In Chapter
One, a second kind of information was discussed: information on the educational environments to which the student is
exposed. Probably the most important aspect of the environment, in the current organization of schools, is the teacher.
Information on teachers is ordinarily maintained in files that
are wholly unassociated with student performance files. Most
data on teachers are maintained at the district level, where
hiring occurs, rather than at the school level. Only the
teacher performance data subsequent to hiring are regularly
maintained at the school level—and such performance data
are ordinarily of little use, recorded only during an initial
probationary period and based on vague criteria, subjective
judgments, and inadequate observation.

In many school districts, however, objective data on
teachers are obtained at the time of hiring, through the
employment application form and standardized teacher
examinations. Such data constitute reasonably good measures
of aspects of the environment to which students of that
teacher are exposed, and with appropriate linking of data at
different levels, can be used for such a purpose, providing
information of types 4, 5, and 6 in Table 1.

Data on other aspects of the educational environment of
a child, such as the curriculum and textbooks to which he is
exposed, the size of classes, school equipment and facilities,
and expenditure information, are generated at either the
school or district level, and maintained at the district and

state levels. Information required by state departments of education (principally expenditures, but also aggregate measures of other items, such as average class size, teacher preparation, and various equipment) is maintained well; information not required by the state is less well maintained. *All such information is maintained fully separate from student records containing student performance data.* Consequently, explicit linkage of these data to student performance data is necessary if the information is to be useful for educational decisions. When such linkage is made, the information that can be generated is of types 4, 5, and 6 in Table 1.

An overall tabulation of types of data generated and maintained relevant to educational decisions is given in Table 4. The rows of the table show types of data that are generated, and the columns show the locus which is the source of the data, and the locus at which files are maintained in unaggregated form. The letter "S" is used to indicate the locus at which the data originate, and the letter "M" is used to indicate the locus at which the data are maintained in unaggregated form. Subscripts are added when the data may originate or be maintained at more than one locus; and parentheses in three cases around "M" indicate that such maintenance sometimes occurs, but is rare. The right-hand column of the table shows the adequacy with which files are maintained for each type of data, with 0 indicating no maintenance, and 1 indicating fully adequate maintenance. The estimates are very rough, and give a combined indication of the frequency with which such files are maintained, and the quality of the data.

The table shows where problems arise at this stage: when data files are maintained at different locations than those at which the data are generated. This involves a physical transfer from one location to another: from the classroom to the school's administrative office; from the school's administrative office to the district administrative office; from the district administrative office to the state department of education; from the state department to the United States Office of Education. The transfers from one location to another are most routine when they are upward along an organizational line of authority, within the school district. They become more problematic when they are upward to a higher level of government, but this becomes rather routine when the higher level of government makes funds conditional upon receipt of the information, as do state education departments. Where the transfers become most problematic, however, is along a path that is neither of these. As a simple example, elementary schools very seldom receive information on their students in secondary schools, even when the secondary schools are part of the same school district. Such an information flow requires either transfer of information up from the secondary schools to the district office, and then back down to the elementary school from the district, or else across organizational lines, directly from secondary schools to the elementary school. Other examples of problematic transfers are data flows from colleges or places of employment to high schools (except for the original application to colleges, for which the high school must send transcripts). Such information is important for examining the longer-range performance of students, and thus through analysis the effect of the school upon them. Yet such data are rarely obtained, except for special projects in which the school follows a particular year's graduates for a short period of time. These transfers of data in directions other than

Generation and Maintenance of Data Necessary for Educational Decisions Related to Student Performance

Locus of data source (S) and file maintenance (M)

	Homeroom or Classroom	School	District	State or Federal	College	Adequacy of File Maintenance
Student Data						
Background	S	M_1				0.6
Course Schedule	S	S, M	(M_2)			1.0
Semester Grades	S	M_1	(M_2)			1.0
Within-Semester Grades	S					0.0
Attendance	S	M				1.0
Standard Test Scores	S	M_1	S, (M_2)			1.0
Extra-curricular	S	M				0.5
Secondary School Performance (Elementary)		S, M				0.1
College Application (Secondary)		S, M				0.5
College Admission (Secondary)					S	0.1
College History (Secondary)					S	0.1
Work History (Secondary)				S		0.0
Teacher Data						
Background, preparation			S, M			0.8
Application Test Score			S, M			0.5
Course Schedule		S, M	M_2			0.5
Performance Ratings		S, M				
Salaries			S, M			1.0
Program Data						
Textbooks, Curriculum		S_1	S_2	S_3		0.0
Pupil-Teacher Ratio or Class Size		S	M			0.8
Library and Other Equip.		S_1, M_1	S_2, M_2			0.8
Current and Capital Expenditures			S, M			1.0

upward along authority lines are rare, sometimes because they are technically more difficult, but also because there is not sufficient organizational incentive for them. There is, however, a balance between incentive and technical difficulties: if the incentive is present but weak, a reduction of technical difficulties can greatly increase the data flow.

It is in this context that a recent development in technology is especially relevant. Probably the most important development in computer technology in the past several years is direct access to remote, electronically stored files by multiple users. This development involves the use of time-shared systems and remote input-output equipment. Such a system is ideally suited to dispersed data-origination and data-use described in Table 2, and implied by any multi-level information system, for it eliminates the need for physical transfer of data from one location to another. Indeed, it is only the existence and economic feasibility of such remote-access systems that make possible a multi-level information system of the sort under consideration here. Typical "management information systems" provide only for upward flow of information along organizational authority lines, and access to information dictated by such lines, ordinarily single access at the top, where the "decision-maker" is to be found. Such a conception of decision-making is compatible with the central, single-access computer. In educational systems, decision-makers should be located at many points in and outside the formal organization. For such decision structures, *remote-access, multiple-user computer systems* provide the appropriate technology.

Control of Data Files and Access to Them
The commercial availability of electronic files with

remote accessibility at prices that make them economically feasible provides a technical solution to data transfer for multi-level information systems. The problems of control of files and access to them are problems of a different sort. In an hierarchical authority system, the problem is resolved by lines of authority, and only under special conditions are data accessible from below or across authority jurisdictions. However, in the emerging structure of public education, individual citizens, state departments of education, state and federal legislatures, and federal agencies, none of which are within the organizational hierarchy, are exercising claims for rights of access to educational information; and since public education is ultimately responsible to the public, many of these claims have the weight of legitimacy. It is far from certain what rules of access will ultimately emerge as technical feasibility increases the urgency of such explicit rules; but two patterns appear as possible alternatives, only one of which is fully compatible with the multi-level decision system under consideration here. This is the concept of a disinterested party, outside the educational system and bonded to insure accountability, acting as an information-banker.

The Concept of an Educational Information-Banker

If an information system of the sort discussed in this book is to be implemented, it implies a role which is new in education, and perhaps in society generally. None of the interested parties who must make educational decisions, from the federal government down to the family, has a right of access to all information files; yet all parties have need of information created at other levels by other interested parties. Thus no one of the interested parties can legitimately be the repository for the information necessary to each party. Most of the information is generated either at the level of the school or at the level of the classroom; but even the parties at these levels—principals and teachers—need information from other schools and other classrooms for the decisions they must make. Quite apart from the needs of other parties for the information currently maintained at the school level, those within the school need a broader information base for many of their decisions.

Thus a role of "information-banker" is necessary in order to receive information from various input sources and make available to each party the information to which it has legitimate access, after appropriate aggregation and analysis. Such an information-banker must have a number of functions if it is to carry out such a role adequately. These functions are very similar to those of a money-banker, although certain initial design functions, (a) and (b) below, are necessitated by the fact that such a role is a new one. The necessary functions are:

(a) Create the design for an information system which receives information from various sources, processes the information in appropriate ways, and provides output information to interested parties.

(b) Assist in the design of any satellite data systems, as in individual school districts or even schools, to insure compatibility with, and automatic inputs to, the information bank.

(c) Monitor inputs to the information bank from each source, to insure quality and quantity of information.

(d) Maintain necessary information bank or files, with security against illegitimate access.

(e) Provide to each of the interested parties that

information to which it has legitimate access, after processing to make it relevant to the decisions of that party.

This role will necessarily evolve in some ways that cannot be presently foreseen; what is important is the basic concept of the role: a disinterested party, which receives input data from sources at which it is generated, protects this information from illegitimate access, processes it, and makes it available in useful form to aid decisions of various parties. There will undoubtedly emerge institutional safeguards to such a service, just as in the case of banking: bonded employees, insurance against violations of security, and similar mechanisms. However, the conflicts of interest and security problems are not the most critical ones in development of this role; most of the information is not of interest to those parties who will not have legitimate access to it. The most critical problems are the technical ones of development of appropriate procedures for assuring input, analysis, and presentation of information so that it is available and useful for educational decisions.

The second possible pattern for information systems in education is a steady movement toward centralization of information, first at the school district level, then at the state and possibly federal levels. Sophisticated data systems, with large capital expenditures for computer equipment, cannot be designed and maintained at the school level, nor at the level of the small district. In addition, the demand of higher levels (state and federal) for performance, program, and expenditure information to aid their decisions exerts a continuing pressure for centralization of file maintenance.

The consequence of such a drift toward centralization of information is a steady erosion of power at lower levels within the educational system: the teacher relative to the principal, then the principal relative to the district superintendent, then the district superintendent relative to the state superintendent, and finally the state superintendent relative to the United States Office of Education. The resentment of each level toward the increasing demands of the next higher level for information is already apparent: the state education departments toward U.S.O.E., the districts toward the state, the principals toward the districts, and the teachers toward the principal.

Despite this resentment, it is the new demands of those outside the educational hierarchy for information about performance—parents, state legislatures, Congress—which make the emergence of the new role of information-banker an especially likely one. For there are no grounds within a bureaucratic organization for legitimacy of access to information except upward along the lines of authority. In contrast, those outside a public bureaucracy who individually constitute its involuntary clients can demand certain information that directly affects them (such as performance information concerning their child); and those same persons, collectively constituting the owners of the public bureaucracy, can—with even stronger claims to legitimacy—demand more general information about the performance of the organization, through their organs of representative government. It is through these channels, that is, through legislation, that the rules governing availability, access, and control of information, and the role-definition of information-banker should emerge. A legislative committee is probably the most appropriate arena for the interests of various parties to shape the rules under which such a system should operate.

A note on security procedures in time-shared systems: One of the major problems that must be solved in any computer system with multiple access to a set of files (a characteristic of all time-sharing systems) is that of file security, restricting access to a specified set of users. Commercial time-sharing firms have developed rather elaborate security systems, for some of their users file information that could be of great interest to other users. These security systems take either of two general forms: systems which restrict file access to a particular set of terminal devices, which have identifying codes built into the hardware; and systems which restrict file access to a particular set of persons, independent of the terminal device, who may unlock the file through use of a particular code word, entered into the input device. The first is comparable to a physical lock opened with a key; the second is comparable to a physical lock opened with a combination. For physical files, neither of these devices is fully satisfactory; but they are the best means devised for security. The procedures for file security in computers, at the present stage of development, seem no worse and no better (except that access cannot be obtained purely through physical force, as in dynamiting a safe) than the methods for physical file security. They are not perfect, but no security system is, and they carry no unique hazards not shared by physical file systems.

Comparability of Data from Different Schools and School Districts

Many of the fruits of an information system of the sort under consideration here cannot be realized within the confines of a given school district. Yet, at present, it is only within the confines of a district that data comparability is maintained, because each district is a distinct administrative unit. Because of the pressure toward information-flow upward to the state level, increasing comparability is being developed among districts in a state. This is part of the general pressure toward centralization described in the preceding section, and will result in increasing information-access from above, but not down, across, or outside the organization.

Yet if teachers, principals, district superintendents, and parents are to be able to use such an information system to aid decisions, data from a number of classrooms, schools, and districts must be brought to bear on the decisions. As was indicated in Chapter One, each of these parties makes decisions involving the second row of Table 1, cells 4, 5, or 6. This row of the table uses information about characteristics of educational environments in relation to student performance. By its very nature, such analysis requires information from many different environments, and not a particular environment, as in row 1 of the table. At the lowest level, information is necessary from many classrooms, to enable abstraction of characteristics of the classroom environment, and to relate those characteristics to student performance in these classrooms; from different schools, to relate school characteristics to performance; and from different districts, to relate characteristics of programs and curricula that differ only between districts to performance. Information most important to the party at a given level is information concerning that level across environments with different characteristics. The teacher needs information about effects of class activity characteristics which may differ from her own; the principal needs information about effects of school characteristics; and the district superintendent needs information about effects of program characteristics that differ only between districts in the community.

To establish such comparability requires an information system that transcends districts, such as that implied by the information-banker concept discussed above. The technical and organizational problems of developing such data comparability are not unique to the system under consideration; their resolution will follow upon the establishment of an organization framework by which a multi-level information system is to be implemented.

Incomplete Information

The data which are best maintained in schools are data on student performance. But an information system appropriate to education decisions requires merging performance data with educational environment data. Data on educational environments are data of the sort listed in the bottom parts of Table 4: data on teacher characteristics, program, curriculum, and facilities characteristics. The maintenance and processing of those data were not discussed in Chapter Two, because of the limitations of the present investigation, and because the patterns of data maintenance are more variable among districts. But in implementation of a multi-level decision system, detailed consideration of those data, and the means by which they can be merged with student performance data to bring information to bear on educational decisions at all levels, is necessary.

In carrying out such a design, it will become apparent that certain data necessary for decisions are not regularly maintained. For example, in many districts, information on size of each class is lost after the current semester or year. Other types of information may not even be obtained at any time. For example, certain family background information, such as father's occupation, is often obtained only at one point in the child's school history, and never updated. Parents' education is obtained in fewer systems, and by methods which provide uncertain reliability.

Still other information may never be obtained as part of administrative data systems, though it is valuable for a multi-level information system. Regular surveys of teacher morale, for example, are almost nonexistent in school systems. The obtaining of such data for input to an information system is highly problematic. It will very likely not be generated unless mandated by a governmental authority, such as a state legislature; and it very likely should not be, unless one of the parties to education can make a strong enough case for such information to bring about such governmental mandate—for the generation of such information is an administrative burden which should not be undertaken on a regular basis unless it is a definite aid to educational decisions.

In general, it is sufficient at this point to be alert to the problem of missing data, and the fact that the problem is not automatically solved by a remote-access multiple-user data system. Certain standards for quantity and quality of information must be established through negotiation by the various interested parties.

Another kind of missing information is information generated outside the public school system, such as information on work and college experience. Such information is of direct interest to principals and superintendents; it provides information on the strengths and weaknesses of various school curricula on which further education or work performance is based; and it provides information valuable for guidance of students currently in school.

Although college records of students are not conceived as a direct part of the information system under consideration here, information from college records could be incorporated for most students who attend college. Most college attendance is within a short distance from home. The incorporation of graduates' performance in nearby colleges into information systems of the sort considered here is certainly feasible. More generally, the automation of administrative functions in colleges will make far easier than at present the automatic reporting of student performance back to high schools. A few colleges currently make such reports; undoubtedly, the number will increase.

Reporting of high school graduates' work history is problematic, and at first would appear impossible. However, it is possible to obtain earnings histories for groups of high school graduates from the Social Security Administration, using procedures which prevent identification of individuals. At least one research project has used this method to examine employment and income histories of graduates of particular high schools. In a multi-level information system maintained by an information-banker, it is likely that procedures for regular reporting of earnings for groups of graduates (grouped according to criteria of interest to the schools) could be established.

Aggregation and Analysis

Only for information on the performance of individual students, in column 1 of Table 1, which is necessary for decisions about individual students, are performance data in unaggregated form required. And only for information about the success of particular educational environments, in row 1 of the table, are environmental data in unaggregated form

necessary. Data which are unaggregated both on the performance side and the environment side are useful only for
decisions requiring information of type 1 in Table 1. Yet files
as maintained and used by schools are unaggregated on both
sides; for example, a student cumulative record which shows
his performance in a particular class. This limits the useful-
ness of such a record to decisions involving that student in
that class. For many educational decisions, information on
particular students or particular programs is not necessary
nor even relevant. Information must at some stage be
aggregated before it is relevant to decisions that go beyond
individual students or programs. The questions, then, concern
the stages at which aggregation should occur, and the
methods of aggregation. The usual pattern of information-
aggregation in school organization at present is that information held at a given level is aggregated to the level just below.
Schools maintain data on individual student performance;
districts maintain performance data aggregated as school
averages; states maintain performance data aggregated as
district averages. This rule of thumb holds as well for data on
educational environments: schools maintain data on class
sizes; districts receive and maintain data on average class size
by school; states maintain data on average class size by
district. When information is released to the public, it is in
the form of school averages when released by the district, and
district averages when released by the state. (Information is
ordinarily not released by the school principal except for
individual student information to the parent, for he usually
has no authority to do so.)

A second characteristic of such data-aggregation is that
it is nearly always carried out separately for individual
variables. For example, student performance data are aggre-

gated to give an average score; and class size is aggregated to give average class size. When data on state-mandated tests in California were published in 1968, district percentile test scores at grades 1, 3, 6, and 10, percent minority students in the district, and pupil-teacher ratio in the district were listed for each district.

This mode of aggregation is of extremely low utility for educational decisions. As a simple example, the percentile test scores at grades 1, 3, 6, and 10 reported in California invite inferences about changes in performance over the years of school between grades 1 and 10. For example, in the published California data in 1968, Oakland had percentile scores of 49, 40, 33, and 31 at grades 1, 3, 6, and 10. The inference of a decline in performance is invited by these scores; but the apparent decline could be entirely due to other reasons. If parents of high-achieving students moved out of the city as these students approached junior high and high school age—a not-unlikely possibility—an aggregate result of this sort could be obtained even if the percentile scores of those who stayed in the Oakland system were *increasing* in percentile score over grades 1-10.

Such presentation also invites unwarranted inferences about effects of educational environments upon performance. The presentation of average pupil-teacher ratios in juxtaposition with average performance scores invites unwarranted inferences about the effect of pupil-teacher ratio on performance.

The lack of utility of data aggregated to the level just below and on a variable-by-variable basis means that for serious inferences about effects of school environments intended to be useful for policy decisions, special "research projects" are necessary, which at great labor and expense collect unaggregated data on subject performance and environments, and process these data in order to answer the research questions. If the correct system of data maintenance and aggregation were carried out to begin with, such special research proejcts would seldom be necessary.*

The technical question then becomes, what is a more appropriate way for data processing, file maintenance, and aggregation to occur? The answer is given by attention to two principles: (1) *Data on each variable must be maintained at levels of disaggregation far below the level to which aggregation is desired, often at the level of the individual student, whose performance and educational environment are recorded;* and (2) *aggregation must be carried out by joint use of more than one variable.*

The design for appropriate data-linkage and file-maintenance is discussed in Chapter Four; in this chapter, it will be useful only to give a few examples by which current data-aggregation and data presentation would be improved by correct procedures. As a first example, the appropriate way for test scores at grades 1, 3, 6, and 10 to be presented (to use the example of published California data) to allow inferences about decline or gain over the years of school is through a method of population-standardization developed by demographers. Although we will not go into technical matters in detail here, it is useful to give the outline of the way such a method operates, to give a feel for the disparity between current methods and correct methods.

*One effect of this would be to put academic educational researchers largely out of work. This is probably as it should be, for many such researchers in the end ignore the policy questions and examine "more interesting" questions which lead merely to academic publication.

For each student at grades 1, 3, 6, and 10, the school has a grade 1 test score on a test comparable to that reported for current grade 1 students.* If the percent of current grade 1 students with a score of Y is X_1 percent, and the percent of current grade 3 students who had a score of Y on their grade 1 test is X_3 percent, then in creation of the population-standardized average score for grade 3, the current grade 3 score of each of those who had a grade 1 score of Y two years ago is multiplied by X_1/X_3. The end result after averaging these weighted scores will be a population-standardized grade 3 average which is based on a distribution of past grade 1 scores identical to the distribution of current grade 1 scores. Carrying out a comparable standardization at grades 6 and 10 will give averages at grades 3, 6, and 10, based on a population with grade 1 test scores comparable to those currently at grade 1. Inferences about decline or rise based on school averages could then be appropriately made. If grade 1 test scores for current grades 3, 6, and 10 do not exist, then a similar population-standardization could be carried out both on current grade 1 students and current grade 3, 6, and 10 students, using other characteristics of the students for which data exist, such as race or father's occupation.

---

*A somewhat different test may have been given, but the standardized score on two such tests ordinarily correlates very highly. The tests should be (and ordinarily are) normed for the same population, and standard scores (mean = 5.0, standard deviation = 1.0) should be used in establishing comparisons. A few students will have missing test scores at grade 1, and should be deleted from the calculation to be described. If a standardized test score is available at grade 2 for the students currently in grades 3, 6, 10, that may be used instead of the grade 1 score.

There is, of course, a conflict between the aims of aggregation to present the actual current state in a classroom, school, or district, and the aims of aggregation to allow inference about changes. The population-standardization described above allows more correct inferences about changes, but at the expense of showing the actual current state. This conflict of purposes should be recognized, leading to the following general principle: *Each aggregation and presentation of information should be designed for specific purposes, rather than as a general-purpose datum.* The problems are very similar to those in index-construction in economics, which require different standardization and modes of aggregation in order to be of value for specific uses. Description of procedures of index construction in economics, and references to further literature in economics index construction can be found in Eric Ruist (1968); and foundations of index construction theory may be found in Frisch (1936).

A more general examination of methods of aggregation and information-presentation to aid in measuring the performance in a given school or program is given in Chapter 5.

The essential characteristic of aggregation of the type discussed above is that it is aggregation of performance data alone; it does not relate performance data to characteristics of the educational environment. Thus it provides information of types 2, 3, 8, or 9 in Table 1, on performance in particular environments or independent of the environment. It does not provide information of types 5 or 6, which aid policy decisions about types of programs or teachers.

In order to provide information of types 5 and 6 that is relevant to general policy decisions about types of educational environments, data processing that goes beyond standardization is necessary. It is necessary to establish explicit linkage between information on student performance and information on characteristics of the educational environment. Referring to Table 4, it is necessary to make explicit use of information in the bottom sections of the table, much of which is currently maintained in different physical files from the information on individual student performance. The possibility of establishing such linkage without difficulty arises through the replacement of physical files by electronic ones, as discussed earlier. The procedures by which such linkage may be carried out are discussed in Chapter Four, which provides a preliminary discussion of the file structure necessary for such a system.

The establishing of such a file structure is the first step in processing information so that it is of use to the various interested parties. The next step makes use of various modes of data-reduction. The principal characteristic of information systems designed to aid decisions is massive data-reduction. A decision is typically an action taken from one of two or, at most, a few alternatives; consequently, for information to be useful to that decision, it must be reduced to a few pieces of information, ordinarily from a massive array of data as a starting point. Numerous techniques, such as regression analysis, factor analysis, analysis of variance, item analysis, discriminant analysis, and other statistical methods comprise the techniques by which large amounts of data are reduced and brought to bear on particular kinds of decision questions.

CHAPTER FOUR

IMPLEMENTATION OF A MULTI-LEVEL INFORMATION SYSTEM

Information Needs of Interested Parties

In order to give concreteness to the way in which a multi-level information system should be implemented, it is useful to give some examples of decisions confronting interested parties at different levels, which would be aided by such a system. Consequently, in the paragraphs below, a number of possible questions faced by various parties will be listed. Information on all of these questions can be provided by a multi-level information system, when fully implemented. Many of the questions, of course, would hardly be answerable with an information system in early stages of its implementation. Nevertheless, it is of value to present such questions here, because an idea of the kinds of questions for which information is needed should guide the development of an information system.

Questions are listed below of the sort that confront district superintendents, principals, teachers, and parents. No questions are listed for state and federal governments; these questions are general policy questions of a sort similar to those that confront a district superintendent. In parentheses following each question is a number referring to the type of information in Table 1 that is relevant to the question.

Superintendents

1. What are the benefits and losses of a new mathematics curriculum, in the long-run mathematics performance of students exposed to it? (3)

2. How effective in other districts is a remedial reading program with a special teacher, and for what kinds of reading deficiencies is it most effective? (5, 6)

3. What is the impact of flexible scheduling, as used in other districts, on the course performance, standardized test performance, and motivation of students, and the satisfaction of teachers? (6)

4. What is the effect of a program of affirmative racial integration on performance of students of different races? (5)

5. What are the effects of a curricular innovation introduced in some districts, such as simulation games in social studies? (2, 3)

Principals

1. How do the various physics curricula in use in surrounding schools compare with respect to (a) the course performance of students as measured by grades, (b) their effects on performance in physics as measured by standardized tests, and (c) their effects on performance in college physics? (3, 6)

2. What are the increments in reading performance among students exposed to different reading programs used in surrounding schools, and how do these increments hold up in succeeding years? (3, 6)

3. Should teacher A be assigned to high-achieving students or low-achieving students? (2)

4. What is the difference in learning of mathematics when scheduled early in the day, rather than late? (6)

5. What difference in achievement and motivation exists between a joint social studies and English course and separate English and social studies courses? (6)

6. How does participation in particular extra-curricular activities affect the motivation, attendance, and performance of students with various types of school records? (2, 5)

7. What is the effect of a poor grade in one subject on subsequent performance in other subjects? (8)

8. How can impending problems for a student be anticipated by an "early-warning system"? (9)

9. Using school grades rather than standardized tests as a criterion, are there any characteristics of teacher and student such that matching on these characteristics will improve performance? (5)

10. Does an increase or decrease in the level of parent involvement in school activities, as experienced in other schools, affect the general course performance of students? (6)

Teachers

1. In a given test or set of tests, what items are missed by a large proportion of the students? (3)

2. What are the characteristics of those items missed by a particular student? (4)

3. For children who are in the bottom quarter of the class in reading, what aspects of mathematics are they doing most poorly at? (elementary level) (2)

4. For the students at the bottom quarter of the class in my subject, what is their average performance in other subjects they are currently taking, and in this subject last year? (2)

5. In a machine-scored quiz devised in conjunction with

another teacher, which of our classes wins in average performance? (3)

Parents and Children

1. How is my child progressing, not merely in his school grades, but in his performance relative to national norms? (1)

2. What is the expected reading level 2, 3, 4 years hence for a student in this school with reading level the same as my child's at present? (2)

3. What kinds of supplementary help are beneficial for children who show a profile of performance comparable to that of my child (e.g., such help as oral reading practice, multiplication drill)? (5)

4. What is the expected grade in algebra 2 in this school for someone with a given set of grades in algebra 1? (2)

5. What kinds of college programs or careers are likely to be successful for someone with a given profile of abilities and interests? (5)

6. What has been the average level of performance of students from this high school with a particular set of grades and college board scores in a given college? (2)

There is also a set of questions that parents and children would have if they had a more expanded range of choice concerning schools, programs, and teachers than they currently have. There are a number of indications that parents may come to have a greater range of choices, through such means as tuition vouchers for attendance at a school of their choice with public funds; released time or after-school for special instruction with public funds; or choice of teacher, subject to class size limitations. If such expansion of choice did come to exist, one of its most important adjuncts would be information aids for the parent and child, to give them objective information on which to base choices:

7. What has been the performance increment in reading by national norms of children under various teachers that my child might have next year? (3)

8. What is the record of a given school in the performance increments of its students on nationally normed tests? (3)

9. What kind of reading program is best for a child who shows a performance profile like that of my child? (4)

These questions give an idea of the kinds of problems to which an information system can be relevant for various parties. In order to move closer to realization of such a potential, it is useful to examine two aspects of the system: the structure of data files and organization of communication; and the organization of equipment required by a multi-level information system. These two aspects of system design will be discussed in the two remaining sections of this chapter.

File Structure and Data Organization

File Structure and Code Assignment

There are numerous sources for the data collected and maintained in an educational data system. These data are typically collected independent of and in isolation from each other. Yet for many purposes, the appropriate presentation of these data involves classification across sources. One example is the classification of a student performance indicator, contained in the student file, by some characteristic of his subject teacher, contained in the teacher data file. In order to present this information, the necessary linkage between the student and teacher must be made.

When these sources are physically stored, this linkage is accomplished by the transcription of the needed data from one source to another. This transcription may necessitate re-ordering the data or casting it in a different format; consequently, when cross-classification is needed, special projects are undertaken to provide the linkage.

With electronic storage of data, direct linkage between separate sources becomes possible without physical relocation. Before describing how such linkage could be implemented, a brief discussion of computer files is in order.

Often in computer applications, the core storage of the computer is not sufficiently large to store at one time all the data required for the problem. In this case storage devices, such as tapes, disks, or drums, may be used to augment computer storage capability. A logical grouping of data contained on one of these devices is called a *file.* These files are organized similarly to physical files. For instance, all the data maintained for students in a school make up a student file. Files are composed of *records*, which are the units of the file accessed by the computer at one time. A record in the student file would typically contain data for one student. If there are 2000 students in one school, there would be 2000 records in that student file. Records are made up of *variables*; for instance, the student's name, age, and mathematics achievement score are possible variables contained in each student's record.

There may be more than one set of files for each type of unit. For example, student data may be in several student files: one containing academic information, another containing health information, and a third containing extra-curricular information. (Alternatively, certain information may be filed by activity, with the students who participate in the activity contained in the record of that activity.) The optimum mode of filing depends on the principal ways in which the files are accessed, just as in physically organized files. However, the difference lies in the ease with which multiple modes of access can be carried out. In physical files, cross-file access is measured in hours or days of search, sorting, and copying; in electronic files, such access is measured in milliseconds.

The number of units for which there are records and the number of types of records may vary widely in files. In student files, there are many students, and a single record or a few records per student. In a file containing school variables maintained at the school, there is only one school but many records; in such a file maintained at the district, there are several schools, and many records for each.

There are a number of ways in which data from various files may be linked. In order to examine effects of teacher characteristics on student performance with school and district characteristics controlled, for example, it is necessary to link together records on individual students, their teachers, their school, and their district.

Such linkage might be carried out in several ways, which will be discussed briefly. The first and simplest structure is a totally nested system. If a system is fully nested, so that each unit at a given level is a member of one and only one unit at each higher level, then a code may be assigned to each level, with uniqueness maintained only within level. Thus for a student in elementary school in a given classroom, the code may consist of his code within class (2 digits), a classroom code within school (2 digits), a school code within district (3 digits), a district code within state (3 digits), and a state code (2 digits). This provides each student a unique code within the country, and allows student records to be linked to teacher, school, district, and state records through use of the appropriate segment of his identification code. The code is longer than would be necessary if he were simply assigned a unique code within the country (12 digits rather than 8), but the code for units of which he is a member need not be included elsewhere in his record.

For example, consider linking up teacher, school, district, and state information for student 15 in classroom 03 in school 081 in district 385 in state 23. The unique codes would be for records at the various levels:

Student	23	385	081	03	15
Teacher	23	385	081	03	
School	23	385	081		
District	23	385			
State	23				

If a system is fully nested, but there is sequential mobility within it (i.e., a unit such as a student is a member of one and only one unit at each higher level, but may move from one to another), then two possibilities are available. The code used in a fully nested system may be used, and changed when the unit moves, just as an individual's street address changes. Or a code may be assigned uniquely across higher-level units, between which mobility occurs. For example, if there is high mobility of students and teachers between schools in a district, each student and teacher might receive a unique code within the district, rather than a unique code within the school. With this coding system, linkage of student records with school records can be achieved in either of two ways: by containing within the school record a list of the codes of all students currently in that school, or by containing within the student's record the school code for the school he is currently attending. The decision whether to use the fully nested code or to embed student or school codes in school or student records is a decision that must be made on the basis of the most frequent types of use of the records.

Finally, a system may have a structure that is not nested: one unit may simultaneously be a member of several higher-level units. For example, a student in high school has more than one teacher at the same time, but not a fixed number. In such a structure, the teacher's code cannot be a part of the student code, since the student has several teachers. In this case, the only solution is either to incorporate within the teacher record the codes of the students he is currently teaching (codes which may be unique within school, district, state, or nation), or to incorporate within the student record the codes of the teachers he currently has (or possibly both, if file storage is less costly than the extra cost of inconvenient access). This non-nested structure is appropriate for many of the activities which occur in education, since each student and teacher is engaged in a variable number of activities.

An example of how a non-nested structure might be used to link data from different files together is the linkage of student grades and standardized test data to characteristics of that year's teacher in that course. The teacher's record contains the teacher's identification code and the characteristics of that teacher. The course code, the grade earned, the teacher code, and standardized test results are all recorded in the student's file. The course code would include codes for subject, course name, course section, and teacher. Course section might incorporate ability-level code, if used. As an example, the code for section 7 of English 10B, 001-010-07-030, would be built up from:

     Subject area = English = 001
     Course name = English 10B = 010
     Course section = 7th period = 07
     Teacher name = Alice Jones = 030

In a similar manner, a standardized achievement test in the related area might use the following identification code:

     Subject area = English = 001
     Standardized test name = TAP-1 = 020
     Time test was given = March 69 = 0369

These identification codes provide linkage between characteristics, student's grades, and standardized test scores, using a procedure somewhat as follows: Find data for subject code 001 in each student's record; retrieve grade and test information; use last portion of course name, i.e., teacher's code, as locator of this student's teacher's record within teacher file; retrieve teacher's characteristic (in this example, verbal ability). Figure 1 is a diagram of this linkage.

File Security System

In implementing a multi-level information system, guards against illegitimate access to data must be built in as part of the file structure. Files may be designated as public information and thus accessed by anyone, or files may be designated as proprietary information with ranges in the amount of access provided. Access to proprietary informa-

Figure 1

Data Linkage

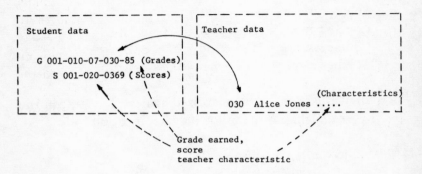

tion is gained either by typing in a password or by using a terminal which the system has validated as accessible to given information.

In some password systems, there are procedures for insuring medium and maximum security. In medium security, the user gains access by typing the name of the file and the required password(s). A maximum security file requires, in addition, appropriate answers to queries posed by the program. For example:

PASSWORD(S) *BARKER, FOXTAIL, CREDENZA*
WHO ARE YOU? ****9*
HOW OLD ARE YOU? *NINETY***
MOTHER'S MAIDEN NAME? *SMITH*

The italic portions are user's answers to questions. If he had answered any of these incorrectly, he would not have gained access to the file he was requesting.

Limits of Access. The passwords prevent unauthorized access to a file. There are also provisions for different limits of access: 1. USE ONLY. The user may use the data under the control of specific programs, but may not gain access to the individual elements of the file. The program may compute averages or differences, for example, and transmit these to the user. 2. READ ONLY. The user may read the data file, list its contents, and copy into another file. 3. UNLIMITED ACCESS. The user may not only read the file, but also change the file.

Organization of Communication

In an information system with many source points for data and many users, the structure of communication provides non-trivial problems. In the system of public education in the United States, there are ordinarily three major types of source points: the teacher or counselor, the principal or school central office staff, and the superintendent or district central office staff. All these source points are potential users of information from the system as well. In addition, there are users outside the formal system: the state and the federal government (sometimes for administrative functions, sometimes for research questions relevant to general policy decisions), parents and students, and personnel in other districts. The patterns of access and the modes of access to any information must obviously be specified in full detail.

In beginning such specification, a few basic principles can be established. *First, each party who constitutes an originating source has a file or set of files associated with him. Second, only the person who is this originating source, who creates and maintains this file or set of files, has unlimited access to all portions of it. Third, there must be a copy operation from file to file, writing specified subsets of the information from one file (e.g., a teacher's file) into another file (e.g., a school file), an operation that occurs at specified times.* This operation should be carried out automatically, under procedures audited by the information-banker. *Fourth, for all users of information, there should be use-only access through specific aggregating, analytical, or administrative programs, which use file information to serve the user's needs.*

These principles are illustrated in a diagram which shows the patterns and types of communication through the information system.

Figure 2 contains paths of flow of information between (1) data originator and data file, (2) data file and data file, and (3) user and data file. The paths are of the three varieties corresponding to the limits of access: unlimited access, read-only, and use-only, respectively. Solid lines with arrows in both directions indicate unlimited access; long-dash lines with a single arrowhead stand for read-only access where the arrowhead points to the destination file; and finally, short-dash lines with a single arrowhead represent use-only files with the arrowhead pointing to the destination. Any flow of data along a long-dash line refers to the automatic updating of a file as a result of a specified procedure. A short-dash line represents flow of data which is under user request. In the diagram, the files at each source point are represented as a single file; but in general, there will be several files at every source point which differ in accessibility.

To exemplify communication along these paths, we may begin with the principal's office scheduling students for

Figure 2

Communication Flow

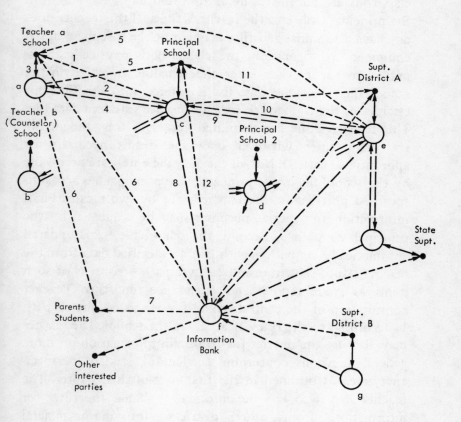

classes. This operation, which results in a file entry in the principal's file, also creates class rolls for each teacher. If each teacher has a file and a terminal, as assumed in this figure, the class rolls are automatically transmitted along path 2, from the principal's file c to the teacher's file a. If the teacher does not have a terminal and file, as might be the case in an initial equipment configuration, the class roll is physically transmitted to the teacher, after the schedule is stored in the school file. Once the class list is entered into the file, this establishes the framework for this teacher's student data file. This teacher alone has unlimited access to this student file and may enter whatever data she deems necessary or appropriate (path 3). Not all the data she enters are accessible by the school file or the principal. The principal has access to specified portions of the teacher's file by two means. First, information for special purposes may be requested by the principal via path 5. Second, the school file, c, is updated automatically via path 4 with certain specified data from the teacher's file. Data transmitted over path 4 consists of such items as grade reports and attendance reporting. Teacher consultation of the central school file is carried out via path 1, according to the rules of access in the school. The teacher may also use the district file to obtain information on more general questions concerning curriculum, student perform- ance, etc., as outlined in the first part of this chapter. The teacher may also use the information bank, the filter for information from other districts, for more general questions.

The teacher's file is accessed by one other party, the parents, who have use-only access via path 6 to specified portions of the teacher's file containing certain information about their own children. Physically, the parents' access would be through a terminal at the information bank. (In addition, parents have access to more general performance information concerning their child and guidance information involving data beyond their own child, from the information bank, via path 7. Upon such parental requests, the information bank [file f] accesses the school file via read-only access for information on that child, through path 8.)

In an initial system in which teachers do not have individual terminal equipment, their information on grades, attendance, etc., would be kept in a gradebook as at present, and periodically entered into the school file through mark-sense cards or similar means. The teacher would use a school terminal for information requests represented by paths 1, 5, and 6, and might maintain a private file accessed by a school terminal. If several terminals existed at different points in a school, full implementation of teacher files as in Figure 2 would be possible without individual terminals.

The principal's use of the system would be most intensively through use of the school files (which are automatically updated via path 4 from teachers' files and via path 9 from district files, and from which information is automatically transmitted to district files and the information bank). For requests involving information from other schools in the district, the principal accesses the district file in use-only mode, and for requests involving information outside the district, he accesses the information bank via path 12.

Use by the district superintendent's office is as indicated by the figure, and requires little elaboration. The state education department's files are periodically updated by district files and periodically transmit state administrative information to those files. In addition, the state makes information queries for research and evaluation purposes as does the district superintendent, through the information bank, using the information to which the bank has access from various districts both within and outside the state.

The information bank is also accessible by other interested parties whose access to the bank is legitimated. These parties may be a research or statistical division of the U.S. Office of Education, committees of the state legislature or Congress, or research branches of other organizations in the community. Obviously, it is necessary for rights of access and limits of access to be clearly defined for such multiple use to occur.

This initial outline of the organization of communication in a multi-user system of this sort gives a view of the general patterns. The details of the system will differ in different applications, and will obviously depend also on the configuration of equipment as discussed below. Before that discussion, however, it is useful to mention briefly two other aspects of the system that are relevant for research and evaluation purposes: experimental designs and data sampling.

Experimental Designs As a By-Product of Scheduling

In an information system based on administrative data, analysis of the performance of students in different environments must ordinarily take the assignment of students to particular environments as given, and use statistical controls to reduce incorrect inferences based on initial correlations between variables. Strict experimental design, with random assignment of students to different environments, is ordinarily not possible, since the school is an ongoing system, with assignment made for a purpose. However, this overlooks one point: many assignments are not made for a purpose, but are made arbitrarily. And when assignments are made arbitrarily, they may be made randomly, with no loss in administrative intent. When a student chooses a course for which three different classes will fit the remainder of his schedule, then if scheduling is done manually, he is arbitrarily assigned to one of the classes. More generally, in working out a schedule, a number of arbitrary decisions are made, especially in the initial stages of the process, in order to provide a frame within which other courses can be fitted. When scheduling is done by computer, arbitrary procedures are also used in such circumstances.

Whenever such arbitrary procedures are used, then the arbitrary procedure can be so designed that the canons of experimental design are met in assignment. Whenever such an arbitrary or random assignment is made between particular alternatives, the assignment and alternatives can be recorded. At the end of a computerized scheduling process, a number of random assignments will have been made among several sets of alternative environments. For each set of alternatives among which random assignments have been made for two or more students, an experimental design exists. Thus a scheduling program may give as a by-product several experimental designs, which can be automatically stored until performance data on standardized tests are obtained during or at the end of the course. These courses may differ in a number of ways: characteristics of teacher, characteristics of classmates, time of day, and sometimes textbook or curricula. By amassing experimental results over a number of semesters and a number of schools, strong inferences can be drawn about the effects of particular characteristics of the environment, inferences that could not be as sound without knowledge concerning which assignments were randomly made and among what set of alternatives.

The procedures used by some existing programs for scheduling students when two or more options are open differ somewhat from random assignment, but in ways which could be easily modified. For example, IBM's scheduling program, CLASS, which schedules all courses for each student before proceeding to the next student, assigns him first to classes in which there are no alternatives. It then moves to classes in which alternatives exist, and assigns him to the section in which most seats remain. It is only this last step which requires change to insure random assignment: he must be scheduled randomly among a well-defined set of courses, rather than according to a characteristic of the course.

The SOCRATES scheduling program does not schedule all courses for a student before proceeding to the next, but schedules first the courses for which there is only one alternative, second the courses for which there are two alternatives, and so on, at each point revising the number of remaining alternatives as available alternatives are preclosed. This program is directly modifiable to allow recording of random assignment, merely by recording the two or more alternatives that exist for each assignment in which a student is randomly assigned to one alternative out of two or more.

Such emerging possibilities allow for creative work in statistical methods. Here is not the place to begin such work. It is enough to note that scheduling programs, appropriately designed, allow experimental designs of radically new forms, purely as a by-product and without altering the criteria on the basis of which class assignments are made.

Data Sampling

For many information problems for which the information system is designed, there will be far more cases of student exposure to a given environment than are necessary for statistical reliability. It is characteristic of schools that many students are exposed to an educational environment that is identical in its measured aspects. Consequently, for efficient analysis of data, it will often be necessary to use sampling procedures. The specific methods of sampling will differ according to the problem; but sampling programs will be necessary to use in conjunction with the file structure described above, in retrieving a set of data for analysis.

Machine Configuration

In order to partially automate school administrative activities, a number of different machine configurations are possible in a school and district, some of which are described below. What is essential for an information system of the sort under consideration is electronic file storage and remote communication capacity. This becomes feasible with little capital expenditure through the purchase or rental of terminal equipment for the school and district offices, and rental of computer time and file storage from a central computer service whose costs are distributed over all users. As will be evident in the discussion below, such a file storage and communication system is possible with nothing more than a teletypewriter, but—because of inconvenient data input and slow printed output—is probably efficient at the school level only with a card reader and remote line printer in addition, described as station 4 below.

Possible Remote Station Configurations

The monthly rental for a modest-size computer falls in the $2000-$4000 range. Such a computer usually is too expensive for a single school. However, the availability of commercial time-sharing services and service bureaus, and regional educational computing centers, provides a way for school districts to begin computer usage without a large initial expenditure.

A computing service underwrites its monthly computer rental and other expenses by renting computer time to various subscribers. A school district, for instance, may rent time from such a service to run a scheduling and grade reporting program. The school district would then be charged according to the amount of computer time it used in running these programs.

There are many services from which a school system as a potential subscriber can choose. In some states there are regional computing centers providing services specifically tailored to the educational area. Time-sharing services, designed to permit interactive use of the computer, are widely available commercially. In addition, other service bureaus, providing batch processing services, are available.

The mode of computer access sets out a range of equipment configurations available to the school district. With a service providing batch processing capabilities, no equipment, or very little (keypunch, sorter), would be necessary at the school, but only activities requiring infrequent computer use—such as scheduling—are feasible. To use a time-sharing service, however, the minimum equipment is a teletypewriter or other teleprinter.

To prevent being too restrictive, a very general computer capability is assumed. Specifically, we assume the existence of a large central computer receiving inputs either locally or from remote stations. Various input/output devices are located at the central computing center, in particular a high-speed line printer, card reader and punch, magnetic tape units, and disk storage units. These devices may be used by the remote user as well as the local user. In addition, the remote user may have his own input/output devices located at the remote station. These remote devices may receive and transmit data to and from the central computer. It would be possible, for example, to request (by means of the tele-printer) that a tape physically located at the central computing center be read and the data be transmitted and listed on the line printer at the remote computing station. These remote stations may contain a teleprinter, a card reader, and/or a line printer.

This discussion will consider four of the possible types of stations for this computing facility. These are built up from the separate components (teleprinter, line printer, card reader) in hierarchical fashion—that is, station 1 is contained in stations 2, 3, 4; station 2 is contained in stations 3, 4; and so on. These stations provide a hierarchy through which a school may progress. All four stations and combinations of these four may exist simultaneously within the system. Figure 3 illustrates the four stations and their linkage to the central computer.

Station 1: No equipment. Initially, a school may not have any equipment at all installed. In order to gain access to a computer, the user must commute to the central computing facility. He submits his job and, after completion, returns to pick it up. The time between job submittal and completion depends on the efficiency and schedule of the computer center, and may range from less than an hour to more than a

Figure 3

Remote Computing Network

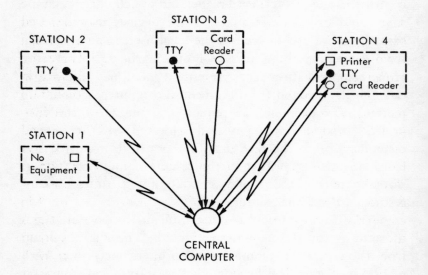

week. This arrangement precludes interactive use of the computer.

Station 2: Teleprinter. Teleprinters are widely used as input devices by commercial time-sharing services. The availability of acoustical couplers on these units allows using any regular telephone to link the terminal to the computer. Consequently, these units may be used wherever there is a telephone. Teleprinters may have a paper tape punch or magnetic tape cassette for storing programs and data.

What advantages are offered by configuration 2 over configuration 1? In principle, all capability of remote usage is available, but the low input and output speeds (typically between 10 and 15 characters/second) limit this usage to low-volume applications. Schools may use the teleprinter for remote job submittal, saving the time and inconvenience of commuting to the computing center. Secondly, all the advantages of the interactive capability of a time-shared system are available. One area which currently is benefiting from this interactive capability is counseling. There are numerous projects which are using computer assistance in counseling. A library of career information, along with methods to explore this information, is given to the students.

Station 3: Teleprinter, card reader. There are several different card readers available for transmitting card data from a remote location to the central computer. These readers read punched cards and mark-sense cards. Addition of a reader considerably increases the flexibility of station 3 in comparison with station 2. When typewriter or paper tape is the only means of data origination, there is no convenient way to record data to be transmitted to the computer. With addition of the card reader a very versatile and portable storage medium, the punched card, is added to the local system. Teachers, for instance, may have their students record quiz answers on mark-sense cards, and receive test grades and tabulations or errors for each item within a few minutes after test-taking. Procedures such as attendance reporting, which must be done daily and consequently have very limited time for completion, would benefit from a local card reader. The local availability of a card reader makes possible quicker service and easier access.

Station 4: Teleprinter, card reader, and printer. Remote line printers are available and would be necessary for printing any large volume of data at the local station. The slower speed of the teleprinter makes this device very poor for printing large volumes of data.

With the incorporation of a line printer the station would be able to transfer all jobs and data to the computer for processing and then receive the results at the local station.

Administrative Procedures for Pupil Personnel Activities in a Fully Automated System

The next section describes some aspects of pupil personnel procedures in a multi-level information system, assuming the existence of a teleprinter available to teachers, and a remote card reader and line printer located at the school office and at the district office. These descriptions are intended to give a sense of the way in which some of these procedures would be carried out differently in such a system than they are with data systems that are manual, or those that use noninteractive modes of computer access.

Scheduling

After preparing the student request cards and master schedule cards on either punched cards or mark-sense cards, these cards are read by card readers at the local station and transmitted via phone lines to the central computer and the scheduling program. The scheduling program uses these data and prints the course conflicts, teacher load, and other available measures of adequacy of the schedule on the printer in the school office. Next, the program asks the human scheduler (via the teleprinter) if this schedule is satisfactory, that is, the final one. If not, he answers "no," but instructs the computer to store his schedule as it stands on the disk file. Then in the next run, only change cards—not the entire file—will have to be read from the card reader. When the human scheduler is satisfied with the schedule, he answers "yes," and the computer then prints the schedules for all students in the school and automatically updates each teacher's file with the class roster for each course.

If sufficient teleprinters were available, the students with their counselors could enter their course requests via teleprinter and immediately learn whether or not the course were available. This system would work in a manner similar to other reservation systems, such as those used by airlines or hotels. Each student would be scheduled as he selected his courses, and changes necessitated by irresolvable conflicts would be made immediately.

Attendance Reporting

Teachers may record a student's absence in much the same manner as in a partially automated system, that is, by sending a prepunched card containing the student's name to the school card reader. Or, if teleprinters are available, a teacher would record absences directly via teleprinter. Master lists of absences are printed at the school on duplication masters for reproduction and distribution through the school. The student master file is automatically updated with this attendance information. A counselor or teacher may request an attendance profile for any student (e.g., Mary Jones) by typing on the terminal:

FIND: Attendance: Mary Jones

The current attendance profile for Mary Jones would then be printed on the printer.

Grade Reporting

A teacher enters her students' grades in her teacher file either by recording them on mark-sense cards or by entering them on the teleprinter. When grade reports are wanted, the teacher requests that the computer average her students' class grades. Since all the grades have been stored in a computer "gradebook," the teacher need not enter these grades. She may apply differential weighting to the tests, and will then obtain summary statistics for her class—the mean, standard deviation, and ranking of students, for instance. After verification of these reports, the teacher indicates that report cards should be printed and the students' cumulative records should be updated with these data. If any additional reports are needed by the teacher, the data system would be organized so that this could be done easily and quickly. For example, a vocabulary for report generation of this sort could be established. To obtain the rank of students in her English 10B class, the teacher would instruct the computer to:

RANK: English 10B

or, to ask for students with one failure, a counselor might type:

FIND: Failures (1)

Testing

Students may record their test answers on a mark-sense card which the computer reads, scores, and stores on tape or disk. Alternatively, the student may sit at a teleprinter which asks the student a question, records his answer, and at the completion of the quiz stores his "test sheet" and his score on tape or disk. Besides the scoring and recording features, in a data system design which includes automated testing, there can be additional capability which provides the teacher or school administrator analytical tools. For example, item analysis of tests may be a part of the testing procedure. In addition, such systems could provide a data bank of questions used by teachers of this particular course. The teacher could select questions and have the test automatically printed on duplication masters.

CHAPTER FIVE

*SCHOOL PERFORMANCE MEASURES**

Data systems of the type discussed in Chapters Three and Four will often be used to answer general questions about how well a school is performing with its students, that is, questions of types 3 and 6 in Table 1. These questions can be studied with increasing sophistication as the flexibility of administrative data systems in schools increases. It is useful, however, to give some idea of possibilities that are close at hand, using current data systems in schools. It is possible then to see the steps toward increasingly specific and increasingly useful questions about performance of schools, questions of type 5 in Table 1. Many of the points in this chapter are well known to educational psychologists; but the increasing use of standardized tests for decisions by educational administrators makes it important that this sophistication in interpretation be more widespread than at present.

Standardized Tests and Their Emerging Uses

Increasingly, the results of standardized tests are being used to evaluate schools and curricula. For example, in response to public pressure, a number of school districts are now publishing school-average test scores, and some states

*We are grateful to Theodore Donaldson for helpful comments on an earlier draft of this chapter.

have begun to make public average test scores for school districts. Federally sponsored and state-sponsored experimental programs ordinarily are evaluated largely on the basis of such standardized test scores.

Designed to measure individual performance, these tests until recently were used mainly for student course placement. In their application to the evaluation of schools and educational programs, however, errors have been made that have led to incorrect inferences about the programs and their effects, and, partly for this reason, some school administrators offer strong resistance to this use of test scores. However, if the tests are valid for measuring the performance of individual students, they are valid also for measuring the school's program—*provided the correct comparisons are made.* It is important, therefore, to examine past practice for some of the errors and inaccuracies that lead to invalid conclusions, and to establish appropriate comparison measures that will render the test scores useful for judging the performance of a school or a program.

The various uses to which test results have been put in the measurement of school performance and program performance in recent years can be grouped under three headings:

a. *Depicting the level of functioning of students in an already existing program, school, or school district. (Type 3 in Table 1.)* This is being done with the publication of school-average scores at different grade levels in various cities, and of school-district averages within states.

b. *Describing the impact of a special program with a definite starting point. (Types 2 and 3 in Table 1.)* Examples of this use abound in the evaluation of More Effective Schools (New York City), Project Head Start, and many other experimental programs that are federally or state financed. Inquiries into the effectiveness of newly instituted school integration, as in White Plains, Buffalo, and Berkeley, are further instances.

c. *Using test scores as "dependent variables" in research aimed at separating effects of student background from those of school environment. (Types 5 and 6 in Table 1.)* This is exemplified in *Equality of Educational Opportunity,* in the "Plowden Report" in England, in the international assessment of achievement in mathematics, in *Racial Isolation in the Public Schools,* and in many other recent analyses. The test score for the individual student, the classroom average, or the school average at one point in time (or sometimes the difference in scores at two points in time) is taken as the dependent variable; then, various "independent variables" are introduced in a statistical analysis to account for variation in these scores between different students, classrooms, or schools.

In all these, such questions arise as: What score should be used (raw score, standardized score, percentile, or grade equivalent)? How should achievement increments, or "growth," be measured? What kinds of comparisons among schools or students are necessary to permit valid inferences about school effects? Because even a seemingly straight-forward publication of test scores for schools can be misleading, it is important to answer these questions and clarify some of the issues involved.

We are not concerned here with designing the ideal measures of school performance, for such a design could not be carried out in existing schools. Instead, taking as given the kinds of tests that schools use, the frequency with which they are administered, and their various uses, we will examine how current practices might be appropriately modified.

Nature of the Tests

At the outset, it is important to recognize that the tests used to measure the performance of districts, schools, or programs tend to be narrow in scope, most often covering only two areas of student performance: verbal and mathematical skills. Presumably, there are two reasons that the testing does not cover a broader range: Some areas (e.g., social studies, history, and foreign languages) do not have the consensus about goals that exists with regard to verbal and mathematical skills; and for some of the other school goals, such as motivation or attitude toward learning, the conventional paper-and-pencil tests are poor measuring devices, and no good alternatives have yet been found. In examining verbal and mathematical skill tests as measures of school performance, therefore, we must bear in mind that such tests were designed only to measure two central skills among those that schools seek to develop, and that they cannot measure all the qualities that schools are intended to develop in their students.

Although the restriction to skills on which there is general consensus about the goal of schools is one way of insuring fairness among schools, it has an important secondary defect: it tends to shape the goals of schools to this narrow frame, though the students would be better served by broader goals for education, just as diligently tested.

The second important property of current testing is that nearly all tests by which schools measure verbal or mathematical achievement are standardized, not on some absolute scale, but relative to other students, and their results are expressed in relative terms. They may be expressed in standard scores based on the distribution of scores of children at the same grade level. The standardizing population ordinarily is that of all the students in the United States at the given grade level, creating "national norms," but there are exceptions (such as "large-city norms"). Sometimes the scores are expressed in terms of a child's percentile position in that same standardizing population of children at the same grade level. Probably most often, the expression of results is in grade-level equivalents (e.g., a student's reading may be equivalent to that of the average child in the United States beginning the 6th grade; he is "reading at the 6th grade level").*

Although for present purposes we will take these tests as given, it may be well to point out that the development of absolute measures would greatly facilitate comparisons. Absolute measures or criterion-referenced tests (which express results in terms of performance according to a fixed criterion) give a meaningful score independent of any population. The use of relative measures means that, as performance levels change in the norming population, either the norms must also be changed (which would preclude over-time comparisons), or the relative measures will no longer accurately express the child's or school's relative standing in the current population. And even if performance levels do not change, the fact that norms are always based on a given grade level makes it difficult to measure relative growth by comparing performance at different grade levels, as will be discussed presently. Absolute measures could most

*Discussion of normed tests and various methods of presenting relative position may be found in texts on educational and psychological testing. See Cronbach (1970), and Angoff (1971).

easily be developed in mathematics, and with somewhat more difficulty in verbal skills.*

A final comment on test norming as it is currently carried out: Because the national norms of widely used tests are the basis for comparisons and policy decisions, some standard for test norming is needed to correct the present, grossly deficient procedures. The tests now used often are normed on small, unrepresentative samples; and even the fact that achievement increments are not equal over the months of the year is not taken into account in the establishing of grade equivalents, or percentiles, for different testing dates. Linear interpolation between yearly points is sometimes used to establish norms for different testing dates in the year. This interpolation gives results which make impossible percentile comparisons of test scores taken at different points in the school year. So long as test scores were being used only to measure individual performance, this source of error was obscured by the measurement error of the test; but when they are used to establish school averages, this measurement error is sharply reduced, leaving the interpolation error exposed. Schools throughout California, for example, administered standardized tests in the fall, and a second form of these tests the following spring, according to which percentile scores were generally found to have fallen, in both high- and low-scoring schools. This result, interpreted as a true result, very likely was due to interpolation in test norming.

---

*This greater difficulty would arise from the fact that language is a product of the particular population that uses it, and therefore differs from population to population. Nevertheless, it would be possible to design measures in which word difficulty was defined by frequency of usage in a well-defined type of textual material, and difficulty of textual passages was defined by linguistic structure and word difficulty.

Deficiencies such as these confirm the need for a set of standards for test-norming procedures, to be developed by a federal agency such as the U.S. Office of Education or the National Bureau of Standards.

Defects and Errors in Use of Tests for Measuring Performance of Schools

The Misleading Use of Grade Equivalents

Test scores sometimes are expressed by year in school. That is to say, a child's score may be reported as being "5.3 years," indicating that it is equivalent to the national norm three-tenths of the way through the fifth grade. Thus, if the child made such a score at the end of November of the fifth grade, he would be at about the national norm.

If one takes the tests and the norms as given, they can yield misleading results in comparisons of the growth of individuals or groups. Black students, for example, are commonly shown to be below grade level, and to fall further behind with each year in school, gaining only .6 to .8 of a grade equivalent per year, while whites gain about 1.0 grade equivalent, consonant with the national norm. The inference usually drawn from this smaller yearly increment is that the schools or the home backgrounds are causing black students to drop further and further below whites of the same age. This may then be taken as prima facie evidence either that the schools are performing more poorly for black students than for whites or that black students are unable to progress as fast as whites.

If, however, one uses the average percentile instead of the average grade equivalent as a measure for these same test scores, the inferences drawn may be the exact opposite. The scores will then show that the black average remains at the same percentile in the national distribution and that the white average also remains at the same percentile. Scores of blacks could even show an increase in the percentile position, while their grade-equivalent scores showed they were "falling further and further behind" the national average. Under the circumstances, which measures should be used, and what inferences could be drawn from them?

To answer this question we must examine the source of the anomaly: the fact that at early grades in school the distribution of scores of children in a given grade (or of a given age) covers a smaller span of grade equivalents (that is, average scores at each grade) than at higher grade levels. This may be illustrated by the use of three tests used in *Equality of Educational Opportunity* that were linked at grades 6, 9, and 12 to allow direct comparisons. Table 5 shows the difference in the conclusions to be drawn from comparisons of grade levels and those of percentiles. The population is whites in the urban Northeast, and we may take the average score of sixth-graders in that population as the norming population, defining the 6.0, 9.0, and 12.0 grade-level scores. The table shows, at each of these grades, the grade equivalent of students who were at the 16th and 84th percentile in this distribution. (These percentiles are one standard deviation below and above the mean, respectively, approximating a normal distribution.) By a grade-equivalent measure, stated in years and tenths-of-years, the students at the 16th percentile are shown to be falling further and further behind, although they remain at the same percentile. At grade 6, they are 1.5 years behind in verbal ability, 2.2 years behind in reading comprehension, and 1.8 years behind in mathematics achievement; by grade 9, they are 2.1, 2.5, and 3.0 years behind; by grade 12, they are 3.2, 3.5, and 4.8 years behind. The same is true in reverse for those at the 84th percentile, who are further ahead in grade equivalents at grade 9 than they were at grade 6. (Their grade equivalent at grade 12 cannot be determined, because the average cannot be usefully extrapolated that far.)

In other words, a student who over these six years remains at exactly the same position relative to others at the 16th percentile appears, by the grade-equivalent measure, to be falling further and further behind. His average grade increment in mathematics between the 6th and the 9th grade is .6 grade per year, but between 9 and 12 it is only .4 grade per year. Yet exactly 84 percent of the students remain above him throughout these years. A student who remained exactly the same number of grade levels behind (i.e., whose grade increments were the same from one year to the next) would in fact be moving up in percentile position! For example, if he had been at the 16th percentile in verbal ability at grade 6, 1.5 years behind, and was still 1.5 years behind at the 12th grade, he would have had to rise to the 32nd percentile to do so, that is to say, of the 84 percent of the students who were above him at grade 6, he would have had to pass 16 percent in order to achieve this position.

Similar discrepancies arise in comparisons of schools. Suppose that school B's average in mathematical achievement is at the 16th percentile in grade 6, while school A's is at the 50th percentile.* The average grade level of school B is 4.2, and that of school A is 6.0, a difference of 1.8 years. If the percentile position of the average in both schools remains

---

*The 50th percentile is the median; for our purposes, we will assume that the mean equals the median and that the 50th percentile therefore is exactly at grade level 6, 9, or 12.

Table 5

Grade equivalents in years and tenths-of-years for grades 6, 9, and 12 for average and for students at the 84th and 16th percentiles, for verbal ability, reading comprehension, and mathematical achievement. Population: White students in urban Northeast (from Equality of Educational Opportunity Survey, September 1965), also used as the norming population.[a]

	Equivalent grade level in years and tenths-of-years		
Verbal Ability			
Average (norm)	6.0	9.0	12.0
Student at 16th percentile	4.5	6.9	8.8
Student at 84th percentile	7.8	12.1	
Reading Comprehension			
Average (norm)	6.0	9.0	12.0
Student at 16th percentile	3.8	6.5	8.5
Student at 84th percentile	8.7	12.7	
Mathematical Achievement			
Average (norm)	6.0	9.0	12.0
Student at 16th percentile	4.2	6.0	7.2
Student at 84th percentile	8.3	14.1	

[a]Data taken from Figures 3.121.1, 3.121.2, and 3.121.3 in Coleman *et al.*, *Equality of Educational Opportunity*, pp. 274-275. To determine the 16th and 84th percentiles, scores are taken one standard deviation below and above the mean, an approximation which assumes a normal distribution of test scores. This may give minor differences from use of the true distribution, which do not, however, affect the inferences drawn from the table.

constant—at the 16th and 50th percentiles—the average in school B will show a grade level of 6.0 at grade 9 and 7.2 at grade 12, that is, a gain of only 1.8 years in the three years from grades 6 to 9, and of 1.2 years in the three years from grades 9 to 12. The average in school A will have gained exactly 3 years, from 6.0 to 9.0, and 9.0 to 12.0, in each of these three-year periods.

All this causes no problem when interpreted correctly. But the difficulty lies in the fact that the very method of reporting invites misinterpretation, even among skilled professionals, and especially among the lay public. For grade-equivalent reports such as those discussed above suggest that students in school B are further and further below those in school A, either in absolute terms or in comparison with other students at the same grade level. But in fact, in comparison with all students at the same grade level, those in school B remain at the same relative position: the 16th percentile.* The grade equivalent comparison is a *horizontal* rather than a vertical comparison, appropriate to statements of "behind" and "ahead," but not "above" and "below."

One way toward understanding the source of this discrepancy is to look at a typical curve for such linked tests over a set of grades. It will have a form like that of Figure 4, which shows the mean curve (solid) and the 16th and 84th percentile curves (dashed) for grades 6, 9, and 12 for verbal ability, using the same data as Table 5. (The curve for grades between these is approximated by straight lines; and the mean curve is extrapolated back to grade 3.) Scale scores, derived from raw scores, are used for the vertical axis, and student grade level for the horizontal axis. To create the scale appropriate for linked tests of this sort, the raw score is so

---

*It may not even be conceptually possible to compare absolute differences at different grade levels, because there is no metric for absolute levels of performance that allows comparison of different segments of the scale. See Cronbach (1970) for further discussion.

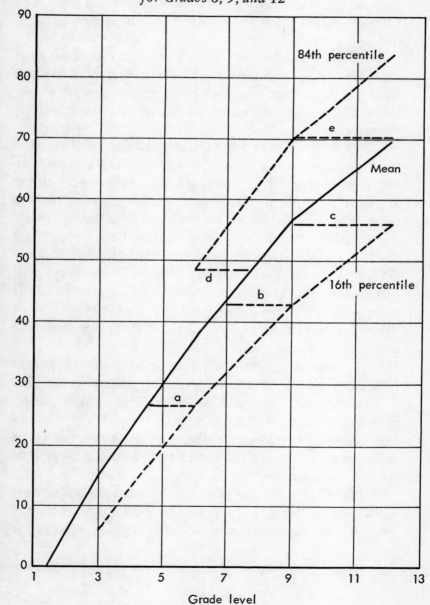

Figure 4

*Linked Test Scores
with Common Mean and Variance
for Grades 6, 9, and 12*

scaled that the variance among students at each grade level is constant. (In this test the scaling was not done perfectly; the variance increases slightly from grade 6 to 9 and from 9 to 12. For present purposes, however, we can assume that the scaling is correct.)

When tests are scaled to create constant variance at each grade level, they uniformly show a declining slope as years in school increase (see Figure 4). Starting at a given distance *below* the average thus means an ever-larger distance *behind* the average curve.

Referring again to Figure 4, we find the "grade-equivalent" measure for a student who is at the 16th percentile at actual grade level 6 by projecting from there, by way of line a, to the mean (or median) curve, and then reading off this point of intersection on the horizontal axis (in this case, 4.5). These "distances behind" (along lines b and c for grades 9 and 12, respectively) increase with the increase in actual grade level, though the "distances below" remain approximately constant. The student's grade-equivalent score is thus a measure, not of his performance relative to the average of others his age, but of the grade level of those whose average performance equals his own.

A "year of growth" in reading at grade 12 is less, relative to the total distribution of 12th-graders' scores, than a year of growth at grade 6. A "grade-equivalent" score, therefore, means a different thing at every grade level. It does not compare the student to others of the same age or at the same actual grade level; it compares him to the average or median student at *another* grade level.

The grade-equivalent score for the school, however, does show exactly what it purports to show: It uses as the yardstick the median student at different grade levels in the norming population, and picks out the grade level at which that median student receives the same score as the student in question or the median student in the given grade in the school in question. It thus shows the *grade level* at which the median student in the school is performing. But it is not appropriate for inferences about the effect of the school, or the *performance* of the school, or the *rates of growth* of children at different grade levels. The absurdity of making such inferences from grade equivalents is shown if one assumes that performance in verbal skills levels off shortly after the end of high school, say at age 20. This would produce a fixed difference in verbal skills, which would remain constant, so that, at age 40, the differences would be the same as at age 20. Yet by a measure of grade equivalents or age equivalents, those at the 16th percentile would come to be 10, 15, and 20 "years behind" those at the 50th percentile as they reached age 30, 35, and 40, respectively, merely because the performance of the two groups leveled off at different points when schooling ended.

Another way of showing that one cannot appropriately measure gain by comparing changes in grade equivalents is as follows: Probably the best measure of an individual's or a school's gain between two points in time is the slope of the line joining the two points on a graph of scale score vs. time, like that of Figure 4. If the gains for two groups have the *same* slope, the lower group will have gained *less* in grade equivalents than the higher group so long as the median curve shows a decreasing slope with the increase of years in school, as in Figure 4. The lower group will be the same "distance *below*" at time 2 as at time 1, but a greater "distance *behind*." If the tests are correctly linked and scaled, however, with constant variance, and the percentile positions of the upper group remain the same, the percentile position of the lower group will remain the same also.

One way of looking at the changes that occur over the years of school is to modify Figure 4 by rescaling the scale score to stretch out the upper end, so that the mean is a straight line (see Figure 5). Instead of a constant variance, this new scale score would have an increasing variance with increasing mean. In such a graph, a particular "growth rate," or slope, is associated with each percentile position in the distribution; if a person remains at the same percentile throughout school, his growth is characterized by a given line. In Figure 5, those at the 84th percentile grow fastest; those at the 50th percentile have a smaller slope or growth rate; and those at the 16th show a still smaller growth rate. Thus, a school whose average student begins in the first grade at the 16th percentile and who at the 12th grade is still at the school's average and still at the 16th percentile will be at exactly the same level compared to all students; but the growth rates for that school and that student are lower than for a school whose average student is at the 50th percentile.

This is not to say that a percentile score is the ideal comparison for most purposes, for it is not. Suppose that two schools showed the same gain (i.e., the same slope in scale score between two grades), and that one school began at the 50th and the other at the 10th percentile. Then, if the school at the 50th went to the 60th percentile, the same gain in scale score would raise the school at the 10th only to the 15th percentile. This point will be discussed at length in the next section. For the present, we only need to recognize that the percentile score is a measure, as it should be, of amount below or above, rather than, like the grade-equivalent measure, of the amount behind or ahead.

Ordinarily, comparisons between schools or school

Figure 5

Linked Test Scores
with Increasing Mean and Variance
for Grades 6, 9, and 12

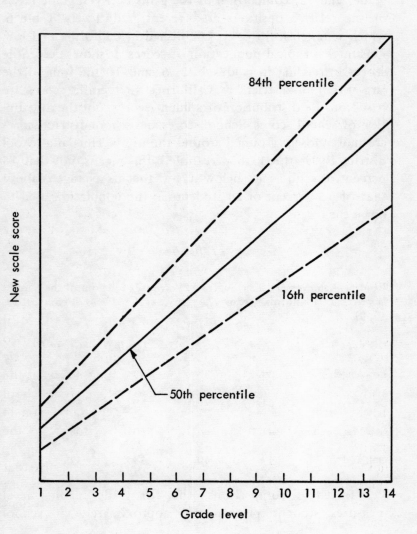

84th percentile

16th percentile

50th percentile

New scale score

Grade level

districts consist of measurements at several grade levels
followed by (1) comparison of the scores at a particular
grade, and (2) comparison of the gains between grade levels
or the relative positions at different grade levels. Table 6,
which is taken from figures published in California in 1968,
illustrates a typical publication of scores. It shows percentile
scores in reading in grades 1, 2, 6, and 10 for four of the
largest school districts in California. (Percentile scores are
based on the distribution of student scores, not the distribution of school scores. School scores and school-district scores
are more closely grouped around the mean. Thus, if a school
district is "at the 15th percentile," this means, not that 15
percent of schools are below it, but that its average is above
that of 15 percent of all students in the population used to
norm the test.)

Table 6

Reading Achievement Test Scores by Percentile for Four of the Largest
Districts in California (from *The Los Angeles Times,* February 23,
1968)

District	Grade 1	Grade 3	Grade 6	Grade 10
Los Angeles	29	37	43	46
San Diego	61	59	59	58
San Francisco	41	36	40	38
Oakland	49	40	33	31

In these comparisons, the first-grade reading level
measures student performance approximately at school

entrance. A gain in percentile position relative to that starting point indicates that students at higher grades in that school system are performing relatively better than those at lower grades; a loss in percentile position indicates that higher grades are performing relatively less well than lower grades.

The Difference in Size of the Percentile at 50% and 90%

Percentile scores may be misleading in a way different from grade-equivalent scores. Because of the bell-shaped distribution curve, many students are clustered closely in absolute score near the 50th percentile, while at the 10th or 90th percentile, students are more widely spaced. Thus, a change in a school's position from the 50th to the 51st percentile is a small change in scale score compared to a shift from the 10th to the 11th percentile. In contrast to the original scale score, constructed as indicated above, the percentile score stretches out the scale toward the middle, and compresses it at the ends. Figure 6, which represents the equivalence between standard scores and percentile scores, shows that a change from the 10th to the 11th percentile is about equivalent in standard score to a change from the 50th to the 52nd percentile; and that changing from the 2nd to the 3rd percentile (or from the 97th to the 98th) is comparable in standard score to going from the 50th to the 57th percentile.

Consequently, the comparison of percentile scores is misleading as a measure of the *amount* of change, although it is useful as a measure of the *direction* of change in relative standing. The amount of change in test scores in Table 6, for example, would have been more accurately represented by standard than by percentile scores.

Standard scores merely change the metric and zero point of the scale score. By creating separate standard scores for every grade, it is possible to arrive at the same mean for the average at each grade level. On the basis of standard scores in which the mean is given a score of 5 and the standard deviation is 1, the scores of the districts in Table 6 may be expressed as shown in Table 7, which gives an accurate picture of the amount of change in the average score of each district.

Figure 6

Equivalence Between Standard Scores and Percentile Scores

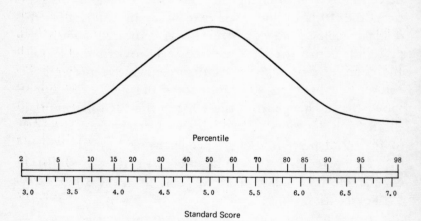

Percentile

| 2 | 5 | 10 | 15 | 20 | 30 | 40 | 50 | 60 | 70 | 80 | 85 | 90 | 95 | 98 |

| 3.0 | 3.5 | 4.0 | 4.5 | 5.0 | 5.5 | 6.0 | 6.5 | 7.0 |

Standard Score

Table 7

Reading Achievement Test Scores by Standard Scores for Four of the Largest Districts in California.

District	Grade 1	Grade 3	Grade 6	Grade 10
Los Angeles	4.45	4.67	4.82	4.90
San Diego	5.28	5.23	5.23	5.20
San Francisco	4.77	4.63	4.75	4.70
Oakland	4.98	4.75	4.56	4.50

Absolute Changes over a Given Period

Scores such as those presented in Tables 6 and 7 show the position of school districts relative to a norm at each grade level. They do not, however, show gain or growth in absolute position. In a school which remains at the 50th percentile on a standard score of 5.0, the average student has progressed at exactly the average rate. It may be desirable to show the rate of growth by the change in scores when different forms of the same test, or linked tests, are used at two or more points in time. For example, comparable tests are often given at the beginning and end of a special program to assess its effectiveness. It is for such purposes that the grade-equivalent scores, misleading as they are, are frequently used.

To make a valid comparison of this kind, one needs a score which shows amount of gain without the misleading properties of the grade-equivalent score. This need is met by a standard score based on a single standardization at the first of the two tests, rather than a separate standardization for each grade (as in Table 7). Take, for example, a program that begins with the 6th grade and continues through grades 7 and 8, with tests given at the beginning of grades 6 and 9. The effect of the program on each student, or on the average of all students, would be measured by the increase, stated in standard deviations, for each student on the basis of the 6th-grade normed distribution. Looking at the figures for reading comprehension in Table 5, for instance, consider three students, represented by the 84th percentile, the 50th percentile, and the 16th percentile, respectively, in the national distribution at grade 6; and suppose they remain at these percentiles relative to the students in the same grade at grade 9. In standard scores based on the distribution at grade 6, their 6th-grade scores are 6.0, 5.0, and 4.0. The standard deviation at grade 6 is 16 points in raw score. The data show that from grade 6 to 9, the student who remains at the 84th percentile gains 19 points in raw score (or 1.2 in 6th-grade score); the student who remains at the 50th percentile gains 19 points in raw score (or 1.2 in 6th-grade standard score); and the student who remains at the 16th percentile also gains 19 points in raw score (or 1.2 in standard score). The final standard scores are 7.2, 6.2, and 5.2, based on a 6th-grade norm of 5.0 standard score. In this example, the student at each percentile gained the same amount in standard score, although as shown in Table 5, the 16th percentile student "fell behind" an additional .3 years, and the 84th percentile student "moved ahead" an additional 1.0 year. Of course, a student who remains at the same relative or percentile position does not necessarily always gain the same amount; if, instead of reading comprehension, we had used verbal activity as the example, the standard scores would have been 7.9, 6.7, and

5.5 for the three students.

The foregoing is meant to show not that grade equivalents are irrelevant information, but rather that they are not an appropriate test for the impact of a program on students who begin at different points. If a student who begins at a low level always gains only the same amount in standard scores as the student who begins at a higher level, he will never catch up; but to assess the effectiveness of the program correctly, one should be able to measure the "catching up" as *extra* gain, shown by gain in standard score, instead of allowing such extra gains to be obscured in grade equivalents.

The Incorrect Use of Ability Measures to Establish Expected Achievement Levels

One method that is sometimes used to determine the "expected" level of performance of students in a given school or program is an ability, or intelligence, measure scored in grade equivalents. The grade level of the ability measure is then compared with the grade level of the achievement measure to determine whether, on the average, students in the school or program are achieving above, below, or at their ability level.*

This procedure developed out of a similar one used at the individual student level to spot students who were "underachieving" relative to their ability. The method, whether applied to schools or to individual students, appears to allow a measurement of expected achievement through use

---

*This is not to say, of course, that an "ability" test, or an achievement test, for that matter, at an earlier point in time, cannot be used in conjunction with later comparable tests to measure gain. See Cronbach and Furby (1970).

of an ability and achievement test at a *single* point in time, rather than of achievement tests at two points in time, as do most other methods. However, this is an illusory possibility, both for individuals and for schools, because of two defects in the method.

The first of these lies in the fact that abilities ordinarily are measured in one or two dimensions (overall ability, or verbal and nonverbal ability), while achievement has a number of dimensions. Further, even when achievement bears a name similar to that of the ability measure, it may be even more closely related to other abilities. For example, scores on mathematical achievement tests typically are more highly correlated with scores on verbal ability tests than with scores on nonverbal ability tests. Since ability test scores do not necessarily correspond to particular achievement scores, we cannot reliably use them to predict such achievements.

Even if there were such a correspondence, however, the second defect in the method would remain: the assumption that the ability tests measure qualities that are not subject to change by the schools. It is a faulty assumption, which can be challenged in any of several ways.

First, anyone examining group-administered tests of ability or intelligence and group-administered achievement tests may find it difficult to determine which is which, except for the section on spatial perception in nonverbal ability. Group-administered verbal ability or intelligence tests are largely tests of vocabulary in one or another form.

Second, when one looks at increases in raw scores on ability or intelligence tests, one finds increments in performance with the increase in grade level, just as in tests designed to measure specific achievement, say in reading comprehension. In the three tests listed in Table 5, the verbal ability test showed a slightly greater increment in performance between grade 6 and grade 12 than either the reading or the mathematics tests. There is no *a priori* reason for assuming that this increment in ability is purely the result of maturation, unaffected by school environment, any more than is the increment in reading or mathematics achievement.

Third, empirical evidence suggests that increments in performance in ability tests tend to be just as much related to variations in school environment as are those in tests labeled achievement tests.

The use of so-called ability or intelligence tests to provide an expected level of achievement at the same point in time thus is not valid. If the school can affect either test score equally, then the "expected" measure is contaminated by school effects; and if some school programs affect one more than the other while some do just the opposite, inferences drawn about the functioning of school programs will be incorrect.

This does not negate the use of both standardized "achievement" and "ability" tests to determine the expected level of performance of each student relative to others in the same class. Everyday performance, which depends on sustained interest and motivation as well as on the skills manifested in such tests, may vary quite widely from standard test scores, so that comparison of the two can provide information about a student's interest and motivation. However, precisely because classroom performance is not measured in standard fashion across schools or even classrooms, this diagnostic use of test scores through comparison with classroom performance cannot be made at the level of the school or program.

Comparison of Measures at Successive Grade Levels

The principal reason behind interest in school achievement measures is the desire to assess the effects of schools on achievement. However, these cannot be inferred with any assurance from measures of school achievement of the type currently available. The essential difficulty derives from the fact that important effects on achievement lie outside the school, and that the amount of achievement attributable to school factors remains unknown. In the absence of a specific model showing how school factors combine with other factors in affecting achievement and how important they are, it is not possible to infer directly from the measures of achievement by school or school district just what the "expected" increment in achievement should be in a school for children who differ in nonschool factors. Suppose, for example, that all schools remained at the same percentile position from grade 1 to 12. There would then be some reason for saying that all schools were identically effective. Yet if a child's later achievement contained an increasingly large component due to the school, and if all schools were equally effective, deviations from the mean should be less relative to the overall mean in later school years—a movement due to the increasing size of the school component of achievement. Thus, identically effective schools, or schools of equal quality, should show smaller coefficients of variation in later years of school (between-school variance smaller relative to the mean performance), the extent of the convergence depending on the strength of the schools compared to external effects. The apparent lack of any evidence of such convergence or regression toward the mean in data on existing schools indicates that either (a) there is a near-perfect correlation between the effectiveness or quality of a school and the starting achievement level of its entering first-graders, or (b) school effects are quite weak relative to nonschool effects. The latter explanation would seem more credible than the existence of a near-perfect correlation; this suggests that, at the current levels of effectiveness of schools, the general expectation for two schools of equal quality whose entering students differ in standard scores or percentiles is that the same differences will continue throughout the school years. In fact, to the question "What is the expected increment in achievement for a student with a given initial score, or a set of students with a given average initial score, when two forms of the same test are used as the initial and final tests?"—a question that usually is implicit where inferences about effects of school programs are made—the answer is unambiguous: *If all the factors affecting achievement continue at the same level over the period between testings as in the period prior to the first test, the expected increment should be, not identical grade-level increments, but an identical increment in standard score for all students (standardized at the date of the earlier test), regardless of starting point.* *

---

*Note that this implies that the variance in scores will be greater at the second time point than at the first, as exemplified by the graph in Figure 5. This increase in variance results from the fact that not all students gain the same amount, so that, for example, there is a spread of gain among both those at the top and at the bottom, increasing the overall spread. If the period between tests is so long as to require linked tests designed for different levels of performance (as in Table 5 or Figure 4), then these tests may have different standard deviations in raw score, making it necessary to create separate standard scores at the two periods. If so, the expected increment cannot be measured directly, but must be inferred as that increment in achievement which gives the same standard score at the two time points.

However, expected increment in standard scores will be independent of the starting point only when the same forces can be expected to continue between tests that were in effect before the testing. If these forces are changed during the period between tests—for example, to increase educational resources for initially low-achieving children—then the impact of this redistribution should show up in larger standard-score increments for the initially low-achieving students (though increments in grade equivalents may still be smaller). Thus the appropriate analysis for the effects of compensatory programs should be the standard-score increments rather than the grade-level increments that are usually reported.

The fact that expected increments in standard score should be identical for all students, and independent of starting point, if all achievement-affecting factors remained the same between testing points as they were before, has an implication also for research on effects of school factors. Often, in such research, the aim is to isolate the effect of school factors on achievement from the effect of nonschool factors such as family background. Given a single test score, background factors of the child are introduced into the analysis along with school factors, so that their effect can be controlled insofar as possible. When there are two test scores, however, at two points in time, the question arises of how to use the two scores as measures of school effect, separating out the nonschool factors.

As indicated earlier, when factors that affect the first test score remain the same between tests, increments in standard score should be identical. Consequently, the results of the first test embody the effects of those background factors, and it is not necessary, then, to include the background factors in the analysis of the final test score. The only such factors which should show an effect beyond that incorporated in the first test score, and thus the only ones that need to be included in the analysis, are those which are different between testing periods from what they were before.*

The same principle holds for school factors: only those which are different between testing points from what they were before will have a bearing on whether the gain in standard score of the school average is more or less than the average gain. What this means in practice is that a first-grade test score, at the very beginning of school, has a very special role. It embodies, subject to its degree of reliability, the child's background factors, both environmental and heredi-tary, without containing school influences. The increase or decrease between the first-grade and later tests in standard scores of children in particular educational settings can be attributed to those educational settings. Technically, a regression analysis which has as dependent variable the second-test standard score, and as independent variables the first-grade test score, family background factors, and school

---

*A caveat is necessary here. Because any test score has imperfect reliability, it embodies only imperfectly the background factors that are also embodied in the final score. In practice, therefore, it may be of value to include family background measures as well as initial test score in the analysis of the final test score, in order to add those background effects that are missing in the initial score because of imperfect reliability. Thus, the effects shown by background factors will include two components: that due to imperfect reliability of the first test score, and that due to changes in the effects of background factors between first and second tests. Because, however, these background factors may be correlated with school factors that affect the second test score, they may reduce the regression coefficients of those school factors. There is some argument, then, for not including them along with the first test score, even though the reliability of that score is imperfect.

factors, should lead to this basis for interpretation: regression coefficients on family background factors show, *not total* family background effects, but *only changes* in family background effects between the two test periods (since the basic background effects are embodied in the initial test scores); regression coefficients on school factors show *total* school effects since the beginning of school, as no school effects were embodied in the initial test scores.*

Standardization for Population Changes

In comparing test scores at different levels in a school or school district, and noting the differences among schools or districts, it is tempting to infer changes from apparent trends. For example, looking at Table 6 or 7, one may be tempted to infer "gain" between grades 1 and 10 in San Francisco and "decline" in Oakland. But it may well be that the population of families from which 10th-grade scores come in Oakland is different from the population from which first-grade scores come, and that the apparent decline is due only to population differences.

There is a method by which such population differences between grades can be standardized so as to eliminate this confounding factor. This is done, heuristically, by reweighting the test scores at later grades before averaging, to reflect as closely as possible the population that exists at the earliest

---

*However, if variations in school factors are confounded with variations in initial test scores or family background scores, this will reduce the regression coefficients of both, and show up as a variance that can be accounted for by school factors, or family background factors, or initial test score. For this reason it may be desirable to exclude constant background factors from the set of independent variables, as mentioned in the preceding footnote.

grade. (The specific method of reweighting depends on the characteristics that are measured for children at later grades and at the first grade.) To illustrate the method, assume that for each of the students now in grades 3, 6, and 10 in Table 7, a standard test score had been obtained at grade 1 and entered in his record. Then, for each small interval of the grade 1 standard score, calculate the proportion of students at current grade 1 who have that score, say X_1, and the proportion of students currently at grade 10 who had that score at grade 1, say X_{10}. Next, the grade 10 score of each current grade 10 student who had a grade 1 score in the interval is weighted by the ratio X_1/X_{10}. This is done for all intervals in the grade 1 test-score distribution, and an average is obtained of the weighted grade 10 test scores. This average is standardized to the current grade 1 population, and may be compared to the current grade 1 average. The average is not the *actual* grade 10 average in the district, but is a better estimate of what the average *would be* if the population composition were the same as that currently in grade 1.

If there is no record of a grade 1 test score for these higher grades, it is necessary to use characteristics for standardizing which are closely related to the standardized test scores and on which information exists for all the students currently in grade 1, as well as those in grades 3, 6, and 10. Where data on race or father's occupation, or both, are available for each student, either of these characteristics, or the two jointly, can be used for standardization if the grade 10 (or 3 or 6) score of each student in a given population group is weighted by the ratio of the proportion of that group in grade 1 to that in grade 10 (or 3 or 6). This will standardize the test averages at each of the later grades to a population base which is the same, in those characteristics used in standardizing, as the current grade 1 population.

The Distribution of Progress

In the measurement of school or district performance levels, the distribution of performance is seldom assessed. Yet such information can be just as important a measure of a school's performance as the average level of student performance, and may be an even more important measure of the effectiveness of a school's programs.

The measures by which schools or districts are ordinarily compared are school averages; but these averages conceal the size of the gap between the highest-performing students and the lowest-performing ones. Measures of the distribution of performance, and changes in this distribution, may be presented in several ways. Of the two that are most reasonable, the first would give both the mean standard score and the standard deviation within the school or the district at each level. If a school has a student population of diverse backgrounds, its standard deviation will be large at grade 1. (Ordinarily, the standard deviation of a school's score will be less than that of the norming population. If standardized scores with a mean of 5.0 and a standard deviation of 1.0 are used, the school's or district's standard deviations will be less than 1; it should average around .9 for a school since about .8 of the variance of standardized achievement-test scores lies within schools.*)

If the standard deviation of a school's standard score decreases from grade 1 to 12, while the average remains constant, this means that, relative to the norming population, the school's students are becoming more homogeneous in

*Equality of Educational Opportunity, Table 3.22.1, p.296.

performance, with both the high- and the low-performing students moving closer to the average than is true in the population as a whole. If the decline in the standard deviation is accompanied by an increase in average standard score, this represents principally extra gain among the initially low-performing students. If it is accompanied by a decrease in average standard score, it represents principally deficient gain among the initially high-performing students.

The second concise way of providing information about the distribution of scores within the school is to present more than one average. Giving the averages for the top and bottom quartiles of the school or district, for example, provides distributional information with two numbers, which is more easily grasped than a number showing the standard deviation. (It does not, however, give the mean for the school as a whole; to do that would require a third number at each grade level.) There are numerous variations on this mode of presenting distributional information, such as giving averages for the first, third, and fifth quintile, or, for more extreme scores, the middle, top, and bottom ninths of the students in a school or district.

The interest in distribution of performance derives from the same source as that in grouping or tracking. If grouping or tracking in a school has the effect of widening the divergence between students in the high and the low tracks, this fact should show up in the comparison of trends in the distribution of test scores for districts with different degrees of grouping or tracking. If tracking is increasing the diversity of achievement in a school, distributional information of the sort described above will show it; if it is not, this fact will be reflected in a nondivergent distribution.

Total Movement in Achievement

Few schools and school districts are as yet equipped to present information about changes in the achievement of individual students without special processing of the students' records. Within a few years, however, many schools will be so equipped. Once such changes can be examined as part of regular administrative data-processing, it will be possible to obtain measures of a student's average movement in achievement. Even at present, this information can be tabulated easily in some schools. In the assessment of the impact of special programs, such measures are readily obtainable because of the before-and-after tests which ordinarily are given to students in these programs.

Whereas the change in average achievement between two tests is the average of the differences in test scores, or, equivalently, the difference of the averages, the measure of total movement is the average of the absolute differences. It captures all movement, up and down, and must be based on differences in the test scores of each individual at the two time points.

This is another important indicator of a school's functioning. It shows the ability of a curriculum to reduce the dependence of final achievement on the initial level of achievement. For example, given two schools whose curricula are highly stratified in tracks, it may be relatively easy in one school to move between tracks but relatively difficult in the other—a difference that will be reflected in a higher rate of total movement in achievement in the first school. This particular information is, in fact, more often needed to assess the effects of tracking than is information merely on the distribution of achievement. It is more directly indicative of the degree of equality of opportunity in schools than are any of the measures discussed in preceding sections. For the degree to which a school is able to make achievement levels independent of initial achievement levels constitutes the degree of equality of opportunity that it provides. This is not to say, of course, that equality of opportunity within a school is the sole important question about a school's functioning. The overall magnitude of opportunity reflected in the average increment in achievement, which is the focus of current measures of school performance, is of obvious importance as well.

This chapter has given an indication of the way standardized tests, as now administered in schools, may be used to measure performance or changes in performance of certain types of students, or of students in certain types of educational environments. Such tests have in the past been used primarily for examining performance of individual students to aid decisions about those students (decisions of types 1, 4, and 7 in Table 1). But they are increasingly coming to be used to evaluate not students, but educational environments, that is, for decisions of types 2, 3, 5, and 6 in Table 1. This chapter indicates some of the common dangers that can lead to incorrect inferences, and some additional measures derived from these test scores that can give greater insight into the performance of schools.

REFERENCES

A Feasibility Study of a Central Computer Facility for an Educational System, General Learning Corporation, final report to United States Office of Education, OEC-1-7-079000-3525, February, 1968.

A Systems Summary Description, Franklin County Schools, Columbus, Ohio, undated.

An Analysis of Regional Planning Agencies in California Funded by ESEA Title III: A Study of the Regional Data Processing Centers, Volume II, Arthur D. Little, Inc., San Jose Unified School District, San Jose, California, 1968.

Andrew, Gary M., and Ronald E. Moir, *Information-Decision Systems in Education* (Itasca, Illinois: F.E. Peacock Publishers, 1970).

Angoff, W.H., "Scales, Norms and Equivalent Scores," pp. 508-600 in R.L. Thorndike (ed.), *Educational Measurement* (Washington, D.C.: American Council on Education, 1971).

Assembly Bill No. 1610. California Education Information System, April 15, 1968, introduced by Assemblyman Campbell.

Bushnell, Don (ed.), and R.L. Howe (assoc. ed.), *A Report of an Experiment—The State Pilot Project in Educational Data Processing,* May 20, 1964.

Coleman, James S., *et al., Equality of Educational Opportunity,* U.S. Government Printing Office, Washington, D.C., 1966.

Counseling Technology, *Educational Technology* (Special

Issue), Vol. IX, No. 3, March 1969.

Cronbach, L.J., *Essentials of Psychological Testing* (New York: Harper and Row, 1970).

Cronbach, L.J., and L. Furby, "How Should We Measure 'Change'—or Should We?" *Psychology Bulletin, 74,* 1970, pp. 68-80.

Department of Education and Science (England), *Children and Their Primary Schools,* ("The Plowden Report"), Her Majesty's Stationery Office, London, 1967.

Foley, W.J., *Data Processing in Education: State and Regional Centers* (Iowa Educational Information Center, Iowa City, Iowa, January, 1969).

Fourth Generation Time-Sharing System, Call-A-Computer, Division of Pillsbury-Occidental Co., Minneapolis, Minnesota, 1969.

Frisch, Ragnar, "Annual Survey of Economic Theory: The Problems of Index Numbers," *Econometrica,* Vol. 4, 1936, pp. 1-38.

Gerard, Ralph W. (ed.), *Computers and Education* (New York: McGraw Hill, 1967).

Goodlad, J.I., J.F. O'Toole, Jr., and L.L. Tyler, *Computers and Information Systems in Education* (New York: Harcourt, Brace and World, 1966).

IBM, Data Processing Application Brief. *Computer Concepts for Elementary and Secondary Schools.* GE20-0327-0. International Business Machines Corporation, 1969.

Integrated Education Information System, ERIC number ES-001-156, DPSC-67-4475, Mount Clemens, Michigan, January 12, 1967.

Journal of Educational Data Processing, Research and Development Center in Educational Data Processing, Educational Systems Corporation, Sacramento, California, Vol. 1, No. 2, May 1964.

Kenney, James B., and R. Robert Rentz, *Automation and Control of Public School Instructional Records* (Itasca, Illinois: F.E. Peacock Publishers, 1970).

Levenson, B., S. Hillsman, T. Rogers, and L. Sanders,

Opportunities of Negro and White Youth in the Apparel Industry, Bureau of Applied Social Research, Columbia University, 1969.

Nasatir, David, *Resistance to Innovation in American Education,* paper prepared for Institute of Government and Public Affairs Conference on Educational Innovations, UCLA, Lake Arrowhead Conference Center, December 17-20, 1965.

Pupil Personnel System, Application Manual, Honeywell EDP File Number 133.0805.0010.0-847, Electronic Data Processing Division, Wellesley Hills, Massachusetts, January 31, 1968.

Racial Isolation in the Public Schools, a Report of the U. S. Commission on Civil Rights, U. S. Government Printing Office, Washington, D. C., 1967.

Ruist, Eric, "Index Numbers: Theoretical Aspects," *International Encyclopedia of the Social Sciences* (New York: Macmillan, 1968, pp. 154-159).

Stanford University. *The Stanford School Scheduling System.* Stanford, California: Department of Industrial Engineering and School of Education, 1968.

Total Information Center, ERIC number ES-001-707, project number DPSC-67-4053, Franklin County Schools, Columbus, Ohio, January 13, 1967.

Total Information for Educational Systems, ERIC number ES-001-447, project number DPSC-67-3967, St. Louis Park, Minnesota, January 13, 1967.

INDEX

Ability tests, linked to "expected" achievement, 103-105

Access. *See* Computerization, modes of access; Information systems for educational decision-making, access and control problems

Achievement tests. *See* Standardized achievement tests

Administrative data systems. *See* Information systems for educational decision-making; Pupil personnel data systems

Advisors. *See* Counseling in secondary schools

Aggregation and analysis, of student performance data, 47-53

American education, pluralistic structure of, *x*

Andrew, Gary M., 117

Angoff, W.H., 86, 117

Attendance reporting:
computerized procedures, 26 (table), 77, 79
existing procedures, 16-17

Automation. *See* Computerization

Batch processing, defined, 29-30

Black students. *See* Students, black/white performance measures

Boards of education, information needs of, 8

Bushnell, Don, 117

California, standardized testing procedures in, 87, 98-99

CLASS computer program for scheduling, described, 72

Code assignment possibilities, outlined, 60-63

Coleman, James S., 91, 117

College Entrance Examination Board, 20

College Locator Service, 20

Comparability of data (across schools, school districts), 43-45

Computerization:
activity list for school operations, 23-28 (table)
benefits of, in school record-handling, 3-4, 17, 38
depersonalizing effects of, *ix-x*
machine configuration possibilities, described, 73-78

121

modes of access, defined and described, 22, 29-31

problem-solving potential of, *ix*

See also Information systems for educational decision-making; Pupil personnel data systems

Consumer power in education, 4

Counseling in secondary schools:

computerized procedures for career and college guidance, 77

existing procedures, 19-20, 22

information needs of advisors, 8-9

Criterion-referenced tests, defined, 86-87

Cronbach, L.J., 86, 92, 103, 118

Curriculum, evaluating the effects of, 114-115

Data-reduction, modes of, 53

Data sampling, 73

Data systems. *See* Information systems for educational decision-making; Pupil personnel data systems

Decision-making. *See* Educational decisions

Dedicated systems, 29 (table), 30

District level, as data depository, 33-34

Economic index construction, and aggregation of educa-

tional data, 52

Educational decisions:

defined and exemplified, 6-10

governmental, 7, 36-38, 54

See also Information systems for educational decision-making; Performance evaluation

Educational environments:

and ability (intelligence) test results, 105

described, 6-7

and equality of opportunity, measurement of, 114-115

linked to performance evaluation data, 35, 45-46, 52-53, 60-63, 64 (fig.)

and nonschool factors, comparative impacts of, 106-110

random assignment of students to, for experimental purposes, 70-72

standardized test scores as "dependent variables," 84

teachers, as prime component of, 34

and tracking, evaluation of, 114-115

Educational research. *See* Research in education

Elementary schools:

first-grade score, special role of, 109-110

and one-way data flows, 36

scheduling procedures of, 12, 14
See also Pupil personnel data systems
Equality of Educational Opportunity, standardized tests used in, 84, 89-90, 91 (table)

Federal government:
  educational information needs of, 7-8, 54, 70
  and test-norming procedures, standardization of, 88
File structure:
  as first decision in data processing, 53, 58-63
  security systems built into, 42-43, 63-65
Flexible scheduling, defined, 12
Foley, W.J., 118
Frisch, Ragnar, 52, 118
Furby, L., 103, 118

Gerard, Ralph W., 118
Goodlad, J.I., 118
Government decisions, and educational information, 7, 36
Grade equivalents, misleading use of, in standardized testing, 88-89, 103
Grade reporting:
  computerized procedures, 27 (table), 80
  existing procedures, 17-18

Head Start, evaluation of, 83
High schools. *See* Secondary schools

Hillsman, S., 118
Howe, R.L., 117

Identification codes. *See* Code assignment possibilities
Information-banker role, defined, 39-42
Information systems for educational decision-making:
  access and control problems
    basic principles, 65-66, 67 (figure)
    centralization trend, causes and consequences of, 41-42, 44
    concept of "educational information-banker," 39-42
    political power implications, 4, 5-6, 9-10, 39, 41-42
    "read only" access, defined, 65
    "unlimited" access, defined, 65
    "use only" access, defined, 65
  administrative *versus* research uses of, 3-4, 7, 49-50, 70
  code assignment possibilities, outlined, 60-63
  communication flow paths, 65-70
  compared to management information systems,

x, 38

data-reduction, modes of, 53

data sampling, 73

design problems
aggregation and analysis, 32, 47-53, 64-65
appropriateness, 4-5, 9-10
comparability of data, 32, 43-45
control and access, 32, 38-43
incomplete data, 32, 45-47
location of data, 32, 33-38
and experimental research, 70-72
file structure, as first step in data processing, 53, 58-63
functions of, and activities related to, 22, 23-28 (table)
interested parties, described, 5-10, 36-40, 44, 54-58
machine configuration possibilities, described, 73-78
multiple-user concept, described, *x*
nested/non-nested structures, compared, 60-63
password security systems, 64-65
and pluralistic structure of

U.S. education, *x*
population-standardization method, described, 50-52, 110-112
and remote-access technology, benefits of, 38, 76-77
types of information used in, 6-10, 35-38, 45-47
See also Computerization; Educational decisions; Performance evaluation; Pupil personnel data systems; Research in education

Integration, racial, evaluation of effectiveness, 84

Intelligence tests. *See* Ability tests

Interactive systems, defined, 29

Kenney, James B., 118

Language achievement tests, difficulties in standardizing, 87

Levenson, B., 118

Linear interpolation of standardized test scores, 87

Location, of data sources and files, 32, 33-38

Los Angeles schools, reading achievement scores, 98 (table), 101 (table)

Machine configuration possibilities, described, 73-78

Management information systems, compared to educational information systems,

x, 38
Master file maintenance:
  computerized procedures, 23 (table)
  existing procedures, 20-22
Master scheduling, 13-14
Moir, Ronald E., 117
More Effective Schools (New York City), evaluation of, 83
Multiprogramming, defined, 29 (table), 30-31

Nasatir, David, 119
Nested/non-nested file structures, compared, 60-63
Noninteractive systems, defined, 22, 29
Norming procedures, for standardized tests, 85-87

Oakland (California) schools:
  aggregate test scores, 49
  reading achievement scores, 98 (table), 101 (table), 110
Oakland (Pontiac, Michigan) schools, data collection procedure, 16
One-user system, defined, 29-30
O'Toole, J.F., Jr., 118
Outputs of education. *See* Performance evaluation

Parents:
  as consumers of educational information, 4, 9, 57-58, 68-69
  as factors in standardized test measurements, 109-110
  lack of data on, 45-46
Password security systems, 64-65
Percentile test scores, compared with grade-equivalents, 88-101
Performance evaluation:
  aggregation and analysis of data, 47-53
  black/white student measures, 88-89
  distribution of progress (across schools, school districts), 112-113
  inadequacy of raw measures, 9
  increasing focus on, 4
  isolation of school/non-school factors, 106-110
  linkage with educational environment data, 35, 45-46, 52-53, 60-63, 64 (figure)
  location of data relating to, 37 (table), 44
  long-range, and one-way data flows, 36, 38
  pupil-teacher ratio inferences, 49
  and standardized tests, emerging uses of, 82-85
  "total movement," as best indicator of school's functioning, 114-115
  types of information used in, 6-10, 35-38, 45-47
  See also Educational de-

cisions; Educational
environments; Stand-
ardized achievement
testing
Plowden Report (Britain), 84,
118
Population-standardization
method, described, 50-52,
110-112
Principals, information needs of,
8, 44, 55-56, 69
Pupil personnel data systems:
for attendance reporting
computerized proce-
dures, 26 (table),
77, 79
existing procedures,
16-17
for career and college counseling,
computerized proce-
dures, 77
existing procedures,
19-20, 22
for grade reporting
computerized proce-
dures, 27 (table),
80
existing procedures,
17-18
for master file maintenance
computerized proce-
dures, 23 (table)
existing procedures,
20-22
for scheduling
computerized proce-
dures, 24-25 (ta-
ble), 78-79
existing procedures,

11-15
for standardized testing
computerized proce-
dures, 28 (table),
80-81
existing procedures,
18-19
Pupil-teacher ratio inferences, 49

Reading achievement scores,
evaluated by percentile,
98-99
Remote batch, defined, 29 (table), 30, 31
Rentz, R. Robert, 118
Report cards. *See* Grade reporting
Research in education:
experimental designs as
by-product of schedul-
ing, 70-72
impact on school functioning, *x*, 3-4
inspired by unaggregated
data, 49-50
and school/nonschool fac-
tors, separation of,
108-110
standardized test scores as
"dependent vari-
ables," 84
types of information used
in, 7
Rogers, T., 118
Ruist, Eric, 52, 119

Sanders, L., 118
San Diego schools, reading
achievement scores, 98 (table), 101 (table)

San Francisco schools, reading achievement scores, 98 (table), 101 (table), 110

Scheduling:
available computer programs, described, 72
computerized procedures, 24-25 (table), 78-79
existing procedures, 11-15
experimental designs as by-product of, 70-72

School boards. *See* Boards of education

School integration, evaluation of effectiveness, 84

School records. *See* Computerization; Information systems for educational decision-making; Pupil personnel data systems

Secondary schools:
career and college counseling procedures, 19-20, 77
See also Pupil personnel data systems

Shared time. *See* Time-sharing systems

Simultaneous access, defined, 29 (table), 30

SOCRATES computer program for scheduling, described, 72

Standardized achievement testing:
absolute changes over time, measurement of, 101-103
black/white student performance measures, 88-89

computerized procedures for, 28 (table), 80-81
distribution of progress (across schools, school districts), 112-113
emerging uses of, 82-85
erroneous inferences from, 83, 87, 88-110
existing procedures, 18-19
"expected" achievement, linked to ability measurement, 103-105
and family background factors, 109-110
first-grade score, special role of, 109-110
and grade equivalents, misleading use of, 88-99, 103
isolation of school/nonschool effects, 106-110
of language achievement, inherent difficulties, 87
linear interpolation between yearly scores, 87
norming procedures, 85-87
percentile scores, advantages and disadvantages of, 88-101
and population differences, weighing method to account for, 50-52, 110-112
school comparisons, 90-92, 94-95
school district comparisons, 98-99

"total movement," as best indicator of school's functioning, 114-115

Stanford School Scheduling System, 13

State governments, educational information needs of, 7, 16, 18, 35, 44, 54, 69-70

Students:
　　black/white performance measures, 88-89
　　college and work histories, lack of data on, 46-47
　　cumulative records of, 20-22, 23 (table), 48
　　information needs of, 9, 57-58
　　random assignment of, for experimental purposes, 70-72
　　"total movement" of, as best indicator of school's functioning, 114-115
　　See also Pupil personnel data systems

Superintendents, information needs of, 8, 44, 55, 69-70

Teachers:
　　information needs of, 8-9, 44, 56-57, 68, 69
　　objective data on, 34
　　as prime component of educational environment, 34

Teleprinters, advantages of, 76-77

Testing. *See* Performance evaluation; Standardized achievement testing

Time-sharing systems:
　　as cost reduction method, 74
　　defined, 29 (table), 30, 31
　　security procedures for, 42-43

Touch Tone telephones, as data collection device, 16

Tracking, evaluation of effects, 114-115

Tyler, L.L., 118

Verbal skills, standardized testing of, 87

SELECTED LIST OF RAND BOOKS

Bagdikian, Ben. *The Information Machines: Their Impact on Men and the Media.* New York: Harper and Row, 1971.

Bretz, Rudy. *A Taxonomy of Communication Media.* Englewood Cliffs, New Jersey: Educational Technology Publications, 1971.

Downs, Anthony. *Inside Bureaucracy.* Boston, Massachusetts: Little, Brown and Company, 1967.

Fisher, Gene H. *Cost Considerations in Systems Analysis.* New York: American Elsevier Publishing Company, 1971.

Haggart, Sue A. (ed.), Stephen M. Barro, Margaret B. Carpenter, Marjorie L. Rapp, James A. DeiRossi, and Gerald C. Sumner. *Program Budgeting for School District Planning.* Englewood Cliffs, New Jersey: Educational Technology Publications, 1972.

Harman, Alvin. *The International Computer Industry: Innovation and Comparative Advantage.* Cambridge, Massachusetts: Harvard University Press, 1971.

Meyer, John R., Martin Wohl, and John F. Kain. *The Urban Transportation Problem.* Cambridge, Massachusetts: Harvard University Press, 1965.

Novick, David (ed.). *Program Budgeting: Program Analysis*

and the Federal Budget. Cambridge, Massachusetts: Harvard University Press, 1965.

Pascal, Anthony. *Thinking About Cities: New Perspectives on Urban Problems.* Belmont, California: Dickenson Publishing Company, 1970.

Quade, Edward S., and Wayne I. Boucher. *Systems Analysis and Policy Planning: Applications in Defense.* New York: American Elsevier Publishing Company, 1968.

Sharpe, William F. *The Economics of Computers.* New York: Columbia University Press, 1969.

Williams, John D. *The Complete Strategyst: Being a Primer on the Theory of Games of Strategy.* New York: McGraw-Hill Book Company, Inc., 1954.

DATE DUE

GAYLORD			PRINTED IN U.S.A.